BESSER IN ENGLISCH

Weniger Fehler in Klausuren

Oberstufe

von David Clarke

Cornelsen
SCRIPTOR

Besser in Englisch, Weniger Fehler in Klausuren – Oberstufe –
wurde geplant und entwickelt von der Cornelsen & Oxford University Press GmbH, Berlin, im Auftrag des Cornelsen Verlags Scriptor, Berlin.

Verfasser David Clarke, Witten

Beratende Mitwirkung Helga Clarke, Witten
Jutta Gutzeit, Wuppertal
Heinrich Hölting, Hagen
Ruth Kröger-Bierhoff, Warburg
Hans-Ulrich Mengel, Hagen

CIP-Titelaufnahme der Deutschen Bibliothek

Besser in Englisch. – Berlin: Cornelsen Scriptor
(Scriptor Lernhilfen)
Weniger Fehler in Klausuren / von David Clarke – 1996
Oberstufe
ISBN 3-589-21074-5

1. Auflage

6.	5.	4.	Die letzten Ziffern bezeichnen
2002	01		Zahl und Jahr des Druckes.

Redaktion Helga Holtkamp unter Mitarbeit von Barbara Swayne

Layout Britta Dieterle, Berlin

Umschlaggestaltung Studio Lochmann, Frankfurt am Main,
unter Verwendung eines Fotos von Peter Wirtz, Dormagen

Techn. Herstellung Freiburger Graphische Betriebe

Vertrieb Cornelsen Verlag, Berlin

ISBN 3-589-21074-5
Bestellnummer 210745

A Zwölf Gruppen von Grundfehlern

B Vierzehn weitere Gruppen von oft gemachten Fehlern

Vorwort

Ein Wort vorweg ...

Obwohl die Bewertungskriterien für Oberstufenklausuren im Fach Englisch von Bundesland zu Bundesland unterschiedlich sind, ist eins sicher: „sprachliche Richtigkeit“ spielt immer eine entscheidende Rolle in der Endbewertung. Beim Verfassen dieser Lernhilfe haben wir eine Reihe von Klausuren mit erheblichen inhaltlichen Mängeln gelesen, die aber wegen des hohen Grades an sprachlicher Richtigkeit trotzdem eine akzeptable Note erhalten haben. Umgekehrt war es anders. Wir haben selten einen Fall gefunden, in dem die inhaltliche Qualität der Klausur ausreichte, um sprachliche Mängel ausgleichen zu können. In der Praxis ist es tatsächlich so, dass *rubbish in good English* höher als *good ideas in bad English* eingestuft wird. Dies mag unfair klingen, aber das Fach heißt eben „Englisch“.

Der Fehlerkatalog

Der Katalog basiert auf einer Untersuchung von 117 Klausuren, die alle im sprachlichen Bereich mit 4+ oder schlechter bewertet wurden.
Beachten Sie bitte, dass wir uns auf Fehler konzentriert haben, die in Klausuren mehr oder weniger häufig zu finden sind. Strukturen, die meist problemlos sind, zum Beispiel das *past perfect* oder der Gebrauch des *simple present* für Fahrpläne usw., kommen also nicht vor.

Aufbau des Buches

Das Buch besteht aus drei Teilen:

A Zwölf Gruppen von Grundfehlern
B Vierzehn weitere Gruppen von oft gemachten Fehlern
C Lösungen

Der erste Teil (der „orange“ Teil) befasst sich mit Fehlerarten, die in der Oberstufe sogar von den wohlwollendsten Lehrern als schwerwiegende Fehler *(blunders)* bewertet werden müssen. Beispiele dieser Fehler sind die falsche Bildung der Zeitformen und die Nichtanwendung von *do* bei Fragen und Verneinung. Es mag scheinen als seien diese Themen in einem Oberstufenbuch fehl am Platz, aber sie sind es leider nicht.

Auch der zweite Teil (der „rote“ Teil) des Buches beinhaltet einige Phänomene – zum Beispiel den Unterschied zwischen *Simple-* und *Progressive* –, die man noch zum Grundwissen über die Sprache zählen könnte. Allerdings sind die Themen fortgeschrittener und befassen sich zunehmend mit Wort- und Ausdrucksfehlern.

Die Fehler Ganz am Anfang jeder Unit bzw. jedes Unitabschnittes gibt es einige typische Fehler. Damit Sie diese Fehler sofort erkennen, sind die falschen Endungen / Wörter in den Sätzen durchgestrichen. Sie werden die meisten Fehler, die in Klausuren angestrichen werden, hier wiedererkennen.

Richtige Beispiele Unmittelbar nach den fehlerhaften Sätzen werden die Sätze richtig wiederholt, wobei die Wörter, auf die es ankommt, farbig hervorgehoben werden.

Die Übungen Die Art und der Aufbau der Übungen sind themenbedingt. Sie finden Übungen zu Formen, zum Gebrauch, aber auch kontrastive Übungen und Textaufgaben. Außerdem werden viele Wörter und Themen wiederholt, die in der Oberstufe vorkommen. So hilft Ihnen *Weniger Fehler in Klausuren* auch, Ihre Vokabelkenntnisse aufzufrischen und zu festigen.
Das Zeichen ⇝ weist auf die Wörter, Zeitformen etc. hin, die Sie einsetzen müssen.

Arbeitsschritte Sie können die Units in beliebiger Reihenfolge bearbeiten.

Schritt 1: Analysieren Sie die Fehler, die Sie in den letzten Klausuren gemacht haben und gruppieren Sie sie nach Art – Gr, T/Zt, W, A usw. – und Häufigkeit.

Schritt 2: Schlagen Sie im Inhaltsverzeichnis nach, um herauszufinden, ob und wo die Fehler, die Sie interessieren, behandelt werden.

Schritt 3: Bei der Bearbeitung der Units sehen Sie sich zuerst die Fehler an. Notieren Sie sich die Nummer des Fehlers, der Sie interessiert. Schauen Sie sich die richtigen Sätze und die entsprechenden Erklärungen an.

Schritt 4: Haben Sie den Grund Ihres Fehlers verstanden, können Sie die Übungen durcharbeiten. Beachten Sie dabei, dass es bei echten Schwierigkeiten besser ist, in den Lösungen nachzuschauen, als einfach zu raten.

A

Zwölf Gruppen von Grundfehlern

A 1 Grundfehler mit Verben und Zeiten

1 Simple Present, dritte Person Singular

① Jane ~~live~~ in Plymouth but she ~~work~~ in Exeter.
② Tom always ~~hurrys~~ home to his TV. He ~~watch~~ it every evening.
③ Sarah ~~cans speak / can speaks~~ good German.

✓ ❶ Jane **lives** in Plymouth but she **works** in Exeter.
✓ ❷ Tom always **hurries** home to his TV. He **watches** it every evening.
✓ ❸ Sarah **can speak** good German.

→ Bei Vollverben hat das **Simple Present** bei allen Personen, außer in der **3. Person Singular** (he, she, it), dieselbe Form wie der Infinitiv.

→ Die **3. Person Singular** von Vollverben endet auf -s ❶.

→ Merken Sie sich die Schreibweise beim Anhängen von -s:
Bei Verben, die auf -ch (watch), -sh (wash), -ss (kiss) und -x (mix) enden, benutzen wir -es ❷.
Bei Verben, die auf -y nach einem Konsonanten (fry, hurry, try) enden, benutzen wir -ies ❷.

→ Beachten Sie: Anders als bei Vollverben haben **Modalverben** wie can, must, should usw. **keine** -s-Endung in der 3. Person ❸.

Exercise 1 Fill in the third person singular of the simple present.

1 The author ______________ the problem of migration.
↝ *examine*

2 The actress ______________ from Berlin to Munich once a week, where she ______________ the part of a politician's wife in a TV series. ↝ *fly, play*

3 In the extract, Charles Lumley ______________ into a pub where he ______________ to get drunk. ↝ *go; hope*

4 The text ______________ into three parts. ↝ *fall*

5 In the final paragraph the author ______________ his attention on women's rights. ↝ *focus*

6 The writer ______________ the problem from two angles.
↝ *approach*

Exercise 2 First look at the German verbs in italics. Then pick out the English equivalents from the list below and complete the sentences. Use the correct form of the simple present.

1 The commentator ________________ the main arguments before he ________________ his own opinion.

→ *zusammenfassen*; *darstellen*

2 In his tragedies, Shakespeare always ________________ comedy as well. These comic sequences ________________ us to accept the terrible things we ________________ on the stage.

→ *anwenden*; *ermöglichen*; *erleben*

3 Laura Marcus ________________ the reader's interest from the beginning. She ________________ this by using case studies that ________________ real-life situations.

→ *jmds. Aufmerksamkeit erregen*; *erreichen*; *sich befassen mit*

4 The writer ________________ that discrimination ________________ huge economic losses. If you ________________ highly qualified people because of, say, their sex, performance obviously ________________ .

→ *hinweisen auf*; *verursachen*; *ablehnen*; *darunter leiden*

→ achieve, catch, cause, deal with, employ, enable, experience, point out, present, reject, suffer, summarize ←

2 Die Formen des Present Perfect

① We ~~have live~~ here for two years.
② Chris ~~has~~ already ~~saw~~ that film.
③ The police ~~have~~ just ~~catched~~ the thieves that robbed the bank.

✓ ❶ We **have lived** here for two years.
✓ ❷ Chris **has** already **seen** that film.
✓ ❸ The police **have** just **caught** the thieves that robbed the bank.

→ Das **Present Perfect** bilden wir mit **have** / **has** + **3. Form** des Vollverbs ❶, ❷.
→ Beachten Sie, dass viele gängige Verben unregelmäßig sind. Hier bleibt Ihnen nichts anderes übrig, als diese Verben auswendig zu lernen ❸.
→ Merken Sie sich auch, dass Adverbien wie **just**, **already**, **still not** und (**not**) **yet** unmittelbar vor dem Vollverb stehen ❷, ❸.

Exercise 3 Fill in the correct form of the present perfect.

1 We ____________ "Macbeth" and ____________ ____________ a new topic. → *finish; now + start*

2 Shakespeare ____________ translated into all major languages. → *be*

3 Please put your clothes away. I ____________ up your room. → *just + tidy*

4 I ____________ four letters and now I ____________ enough for one day. → *already + write; have*

5 Jane ____________ my classes since September and she ____________ well. → *attend; always + do*

6 Mrs Gregg ____________ her driving test although she ____________ 30 lessons. → *still + not pass; have*

Exercise 4 Make present perfect sentences with the elements. You must add articles and prepositions.

1 UK / ask / EU / more time / think about / new regulations / toxic emissions

____

____.

2 Unfortunately / UK / use / Irish Sea / chemical dump / years

____

____.

3 British firms / now + agree / fit / most modern filters / new factories

____

____.

4 Germany / yet + not approve / export / nuclear waste / Russia

____

____.

5 car makers / fit / catalytic converters / all new cars / since 1990

____

____.

6 more efficient engines / lead / big fuel savings

____.

3 Verneinung und Fragen mit *do*

① Jane ~~speak not~~ German.
② Fred ~~knew not~~ the answer.
③ ~~Like~~ you TV?
④ ~~Do you can play~~ tennis, Tom?

✓ ❶ Jane **does not speak** German.
✓ ❷ Fred **didn't know** the answer.
✓ ❸ **Do you like** TV?
✓ ❹ **Can you play** tennis, Tom?

→ Im Englischen ist es nicht möglich, ein Vollverb zu verneinen bzw. Fragen zu bilden ohne ein Hilfsverb. Deshalb müssen wir beim **Simple Present** und **Simple Past** die Hilfsverben **do** / **does** / **did** benutzen ❶, ❷, ❸.

→ Ist im Satz ein Hilfsverb vorhanden, bilden wir Verneinung und Fragen ❹ genau wie im Deutschen.

Exercise 5 Fill in the correct form of the verbs. Use the tense given in italics.

1 Shakespeare ______________ any of his plays in prose.
not write: simple past

2 Britain ______________ alone. The Danish ______________ the idea of a centralized Europe, either.
not be; not like: simple present

3 Those who ______________ with a European currency ______________ to realize that the single market ______________ possible without it.
not agree; not seem; not be: simple present

4 A lot of people ______________ away during the school holidays.
not go: simple present

5 The UK ______________ a lot of EU labour regulations because they ______________ to endanger jobs.
not introduce: present perfect; not want: simple present

6 I ______________ the article very helpful. The writer ______________ several aspects of the problem at all.
not find: simple past; not mention: simple present

Exercise 6 Read the sentences about the EU. Form questions by asking about the words in italics. Use the question words given.

The EU has got 15 members at the moment.
How many members has the EU got at the moment?

1 The three newest members joined the EU *in 1995.*

When ______________________________ ?

2 The other members were glad about this *because these three countries are quite rich.*

Why ______________________________ ?

3 France and Germany would like to see *a fully integrated union like the USA.*

What ______________________________ ?

4 They think this *because their two countries suffered so badly in two world wars.*

Why ______________________________ ?

5 Britain and Denmark on the other hand want *a loose confederation of autonomous nation states.*

What ______________________________ ?

Exercise 7 Read this text about Ernest Hemingway. Form questions by asking about the words in italics.

Ernest Hemingway grew up in a respectable middle-class family *in Chicago*. After high school he joined *the Kansas City Star*[1] as a reporter. He soon became bored with life in Kansas City. He left the Star *because he wanted adventure and some good stories*[2]. For this reason he went *to the Italian front*[3] as a freelance reporter *in 1918*[4].

Hemingway *was so shocked by the war*[5] that he became a Red Cross ambulance-driver. He himself was badly wounded, however, and had to spend *over a year*[6] in hospital. During this time he became aware of the meaninglessness of the individual in modern 20th century society. These insights led him to write *A Farewell to Arms*[7], one of his most successful books.

Hemingway produced his best work *in the 1920s and early 30s*[8]. During his later life he became depressive and obsessed with *the fear of losing his talent*[9]. He produced little of any value until, suddenly, the short novel *The Old Man and the Sea*[10] in 1952. This work won him the Nobel Prize *in 1954*[11]. Nonetheless, he soon sank back into self-doubt and alcohol abuse. He finally died *by his own hand*[12] in 1961.

Where **did Hemingway grow up**?

1 What newspaper ______________________________?

2 Why ______________________________?

3 What country ______________________________?

4 In what year ______________________________?

5 Why ______________________________

______________________________?

6 How long ______________________________

______________________________?

7 What book ______________________________

______________________________?

8 During what period ______________________________

______________________________?

9 What ______________ obsessed with ______________

______________?

10 What short novel ______________________________?

11 When ______________________________

______________________________?

12 How ______________________________?

A 2 Grundfehler mit Adjektiven und Adverbien

1 Der Unterschied zwischen Adjektiven und Adverbien

① You should always ~~drive careful~~ on wet roads.
② Tom is a ~~surprising good~~ singer. He sang ~~absolute wonderfully~~ last night.

✓ ❶ You should always **drive carefully** on wet roads.
✓ ❷ Tom is a **surprisingly good** singer. He sang **absolutely wonderfully** last night.
✓ ❸ **Quiet, mousy Sarah** has bought some **fabulous new clothes** and a **fast motorbike.**
✓ ❹ Simon **is** quite **shy** even though he **seems self-confident.**

→ Im Deutschen haben Adjektive und Adverbien dieselbe Form. Auf diese Tatsache ist der klassische Fehler beim Gebrauch von Adverbien zurückzuführen ❶, ❷.

→ Wollen wir **Personen** oder **Sachen** beschreiben, verwenden wir **Adjektive** ❸.
Adjektive stehen unmittelbar vor **Substantiven** ❸ oder nach **be** ❹ und gewissen anderen Verben, nämlich **become**, **get**, **keep**, **seem** ❹ und **look** *(aussehen)*, **taste**, **smell**, **sound**.

→ Wir verwenden **Adverbien**, um **Verben** ❶, **Adjektive** ❷ und **andere Adverbien** ❷ näher zu beschreiben.

→ Die meisten **Adverbien** werden durch das Anhängen von **-ly** an das entsprechende **Adjektiv** gebildet ❶, ❷.

→ Beachten Sie aber die Adverbien, die dieselbe Form wie das Adjektiv haben: **fast**, **long**, **low**.

Exercise 1 On page 15 there is a step-by-step recipe for lemon chicken *(Hähnchen mit Zitrone)*. Read the recipe on page 15 and put the adjectives into the adverb form where necessary.

Lemon Chicken

This ______________ popular Italian meal smells ______________ wonderful and tastes ______________ delicious. Here is how you prepare it ______________ quick and ______________ easy:

Wash chicken ______________ thorough and dry with ______________ clean kitchen towel. Cut chicken into eight ______________ medium-sized pieces. Heat ______________ large saucepan and brown [anbraten] chicken pieces in own fat. Chop a ______________ small onion, 2 tomatoes and 4 ______________ large carrots. When chicken pieces are ______________ ready, remove from pan. Throw fat away. Put ______________ rough one dessert spoonful of butter into pan and fry onion ______________ gentle. Add tomatoes, chopped carrot and a piece of lemon peel and mix ______________ careful. Season mixture ______________ generous with rosemary; add salt and pepper. Add chicken pieces to mixture and simmer ______________ slow for ______________ approximate one hour. Stir mixture ______________ regular. Add some water if ______________ necessary.

While chicken is ______________ gentle simmering, prepare the lemon sauce as follows: Put one soup spoon of flour into a large glass; ______________ gradual fill glass with milk, mixing ______________ continuous. (Do this ______________ thorough, making ______________ sure there are no lumps.) Beat two eggs, the juice of a ______________ fresh pressed lemon and a pinch of salt in a bowl. When the chicken is ______________ full cooked, add milk and flour, mixing ______________ constant. Take the pan from heat and add the beaten eggs. Mix and return to heat for a few moments until the sauce is ______________ thick.

2 Die Steigerung und Sätze mit Vergleichen

① Sally is ~~carefuller~~ than Ben and she's ~~more clever,~~ too.
② Is Sally's boyfriend ~~how / so old as~~ she is?
③ The green shirt is ~~more expensive as~~ the red one.

✓ ❶ Sally is **more careful** than Ben and she's **cleverer,** too.
✓ ❷ Is Sally's boyfriend **as old as** she is?
✓ ❸ The green shirt is **more expensive than** the red one.

→ Bei der **Steigerung von Adjektiven und Adverbien** sind die häufigsten Fehler:
der Versuch, mehrsilbige Adjektive und Adverbien auf -**ly** mit -**er** / -**est** zu steigern ❶ und die falsche Formulierung bei einem Vergleich im Satz zu verwenden ❷, ❸.

Adjektive:

→ Kurze, einsilbige Adjektive und zweisilbige Adjektive, die auf -**y**, -**le**, -**er** und -**ow** enden, werden mit -**er** / -**est** gesteigert:
einsilbig: **nice** – nic**er** – nic**est**, **old** – old**er** – old**est**, **narrow** – narrow**er** – narrow**est**
zweisilbig: **clever** – clever**er** – clever**est**, **noisy** – nois**ier** – nois**iest**, **simple** – simpl**er** – simpl**est**

→ Längere, mehrsilbige Adjektive und zweisilbige Adjektive, die **nicht** auf -**y**, -**le**, -**er**, -**ow** enden, steigern wir mit **more** / **most**:
mehrsilbig: **interesting** – **more** interesting – **most** interesting, **prejudiced** – **more** prejudiced – **most** prejudiced
zweisilbig ohne -**y**, -**le**, -**er**, -**ow**:
boring – **more** boring – **most** boring, **careless** – **more** careless – **most** careless

→ Beachten Sie, dass folgende Adjektive **unregelmäßig** gesteigert werden:
bad – worse – worst, **many** – more – most, **good** – better – best, **much** – more – most, **little** – less – least

Adverbien:

→ Endet ein Adverb auf -**ly,** wird es mit **more** / **most** gesteigert:
noisily – **more** noisily – **most** noisily,
prettily – **more** prettily – **most** prettily

→ Die Adverbien, die dieselbe Form wie das entsprechende Adjektiv haben, werden mit -**er** / -**est** gesteigert:
early – earl**ier** – earl**iest**, **fast** – fast**er** – fast**est**, **hard** – hard**er** – hard**est**, **long** – long**er** – long**est**, **straight** – straight**er** – straight**est**

→ Beachten Sie, dass folgende Adverbien **unregelmäßig** gesteigert werden:
badly – worse – worst, **little** – less – least, **well** – better – best

Vergleiche:

→ Wollen wir Personen oder Sachen **im Satz** miteinander **vergleichen,** gibt es drei Möglichkeiten:

kein Unterschied:	**as … as**	*genauso … wie*
negativer Unterschied:	**not as … as**	*nicht so … wie*
	less … than	*weniger … als*
positiver Unterschied:	**-er … than**	*mehr … als*
	more … than	*mehr … als*

Exercise 2 Put the adjectives into the correct form.

1 Jane is finding life rather ____________ at the moment but I'm sure she will be ____________ when they give her some ____________________ work to do.

boring; happy; interesting

2 I'm ____________ everybody would work better if the boss was __________________ . He could be a lot ____________ , too.

sure; supportive; friendly

3 The UK is said to be among the ___________________ countries in the EU. The British find it ____________________ than other people to give up their independence. *nationalist; difficult*

4 "Do you think it is ____________ that southern Europeans are ____________________ than northerners?"

"No, I don't. They have the ____________ and _________ _______________ moral code in the whole of Europe. I have read that a ___________ number of women are trapped in the ___________________ marriages, for example."

true; tolerant; strict; traditional; huge; awful

5 "Which of these three poems do you like _______ ?"

"It is ____________ to say. I definitely think this one is ____________ than that one, though." *good; hard; good*

6 This analysis would be __________________ if it set priorities. It would be _______________ if we could do everything at once, but we can't. *useful; wonderful*

Exercise 3 Put the adverbs into the correct form.

1 You make unnecessary mistakes. You must check your work ______________________ . ~ *carefully*

2 Why can't you speak ________________ ? Our German visitors could understand you __________________ then.
~ *slowly; easily*

3 Management says they will pay us ___________ in future but we will all have to work ___________ and ________________ . Some people will also have to work ___________ .
~ *well; hard; efficiently; long*

4 If Jack doesn't take his job ____________________ , he will lose it. ~ *seriously*

5 Of course we can't expect to win unless we train ______________ than just once a week. The best teams are always the ones that train __________________ . ~ *often; frequently*

6 Jane speaks German ____________________ than Tom, but Tom speaks it much __________________ . Jane worries __________ about making mistakes. ~ *correctly; fluently; much*

Exercise 4 Make comparisons in sentences.

1 Germany has about 82 million people, the UK roughly 55 million.
~ *small*
The UK is ____________________________________ Germany.

2 David has got three children and Roger has got two.
~ *not / many*
Roger has not got ________________________________ David.

3 The press report has got about 400 words; the essay is twice as long. ~ *much + short*
The press report is ___________________________________ .

4 I can't see any difference between the AX and the 204.
~ *good*
The AX is just _______________________________________ .

A 3 Grundfehler bei den Artikeln

1 Der unbestimmte Artikel bei Berufen, Nationalitäten und Krankheiten

① Alan is ~~engineer~~, but is he ~~Englishman~~ or ~~Scot~~?
② Mendelssohn-Bartholdy was born ~~Jew~~ but he became ~~Christian~~.
③ Brenda has got ~~headache~~ and ~~sore throat~~.

✓ ❶ Alan is **an engineer**, but is he **an Englishman** or **a Scot**?
✓ ❷ Mendelssohn-Bartholdy was born **a Jew** but he became **a Christian**.
✓ ❸ Brenda has got **a headache** and **a sore throat**.

→ Der **unbestimmte Artikel** wird im Englischen im Gegensatz zum Deutschen bei Berufsangaben ❶, bei Nationalitäten ❶, bei Religionen ❷ und bei einigen Krankheiten ❸ gebraucht.

→ Beachten Sie bei **Krankheiten**:

have **a** headache	*Kopfweh haben*
have **a** sore throat	*Halsschmerzen haben*
have **an** attack of hayfever	*einen Heuschnupfenanfall haben*
aber:	
have diarrhoea	*Durchfall haben*
have earache	*Ohrenschmerzen haben*

Exercise 1 Use the indefinite article **a** / **an** only when necessary.

1 Hemingway was _______ American writer. He wrote _______ number of short stories about his war experiences.

2 David became _______ officer cadet at _______ military academy in 1990.

3 For heaven's sake don't say Helen is _______ English. She's _______ Scot.

4 Sean is _______ Ulster protestant but he is no _______ extremist. His wife is _______ catholic.

5 Germany became _______ federal republic in 1948.

6 I'm not surprised you've got _______ stomach ache and _______ diarrhoea. You eat like _______ pig sometimes.

2 Der unbestimmte Artikel nach *half, quite / rather, such* und *what*

① I'm hungry. I only had ~~a half apple~~ for lunch.
② Ted can be a ~~such idiot / so an idiot~~ sometimes.
③ ~~What pity~~ that we missed the first part of the film.

✓ ❶ I'm hungry. I only had **half an** apple for lunch.
✓ ❷ Ted can be **such an** idiot sometimes.
✓ ❸ **What a** pity that we missed the first part of the film.

→ Normalerweise steht der unbestimmte Artikel vor zählbaren Substantiven bzw. Adjektiven + zählbaren Substantiven:
The Greens have got **a** house with **a** big garden.

→ Bei **half** ❶, **quite** / **rather**, **such** ❷ und **what** (als Ausruf) ❸ wird der unbestimmte Artikel **nachgestellt:**
It only takes about **half an** hour to get to the airport.
We had **quite a** nice time on holiday.
This is **rather a** difficult test for beginners.
I've never had **such a** wonderful holiday before.
Oh, **what a** beautiful dress that is!

Exercise 2 Put the words in italics into the sentences. Use the indefinite article in the right place when necessary.

1 I have never heard ______________________________ in my life.
such, stupid remark

2 Last night we had to wait ____________________ before the film began. *half, hour*

3 Unfortunately Ben can be ____________________ when he drinks too much. *rather, fool*

4 ____________________ you sometimes talk, Brenda.
what, nonsense

5 Barbara had ___________________________ of hayfever in June.
quite, serious attack

6 I had to wait ___________________________ before I could see Mr Gregg. *rather, longtime*

3 Gängige Wendungen mit dem unbestimmten Artikel

① What is it, Jean? I'm ~~in awful hurry~~.
② Please ~~take seat~~. I won't be a moment.

✓ ❶ What is it, Jean? I'm **in an awful hurry**.
✓ ❷ Please **take a seat**. I won't be a moment.

→ Merken Sie sich diese Wendungen, die im Englischen – im Gegensatz zum Deutschen – mit dem unbestimmten Artikel gebildet werden:

be in **a** bad / good mood	*schlechter / guter Laune sein*
be in **a** hurry	*in Eile sein*
be in **a** position to do sth.	*in der Lage sein, etwas zu tun*
come to **an** end	*zu Ende gehen*
do sth. for **a** change	*etwas zur Abwechslung machen*
have **a** bath / shave / shower / wash	*sich baden / rasieren / duschen / waschen*
speak in **a** loud / quiet voice	*mit lauter / leiser Stimme sprechen*
take **a** seat	*Platz nehmen*
work without **a** break	*ohne Pause / Unterbrechung arbeiten*

Exercise 3 Translate the sentences into English.

1 *Birgit war schlechter Laune, also ließ ich sie allein.*

Birgit ______________________________ , so I left her in peace.

2 *Heute haben wir zehn Stunden ohne Unterbrechung gearbeitet.*

We worked ______________________________________ today.

3 *Jochen kommt gleich. Er duscht sich gerade.*

Jochen is just coming. ______________________________ .

4 *Ich habe sehr wenig Zeit. Ich bin in großer Eile.*

I have ____________________ . I'm ______________________ .

5 *Alle guten Dinge gehen zu Ende.*

____ .

6 *Warum können wir nicht zur Abwechslung ins Theater gehen?*

Why can't we ____ ?

4 Der Gebrauch des bestimmten Artikels

① ~~The society~~ has changed a lot – think of ~~the women's~~ rights, for example.
② ~~The energy~~ costs are going up because ~~the fossil fuels~~ are running out.
③ ~~The most~~ people want peace.
④ Harry lives in ~~the Station Road~~, doesn't he?
⑤ Ann has cut ~~the hand~~.

✓ ❶ **Society** has changed a lot – think of **women's rights**, for example.
✓ ❷ **Energy costs** are going up because **fossil fuels** are running out.
✓ ❸ **Most** people want peace.
✓ ❹ Harry lives **in Station Road**, doesn't he?
✓ ❺ Ann has cut **her hand**.

→ Wenn wir **generell** und ohne Ausnahme reden wollen, wird im Englischen der bestimmte Artikel **nicht** gebraucht ❶, ❷.

Vergleichen Sie:
World governments must do something about **unemployment** and **pollution**.
Die Regierungen der Welt müssen etwas gegen (die) Arbeitslosigkeit und (die) Umweltverschmutzung unternehmen.

The governments of the EU must do something about **the unemployment among school-leavers** and **the pollution of European rivers**.
Die Regierungen der EU müssen etwas gegen die Arbeitslosigkeit unter den Schulabgängern und die Verschmutzung der europäischen Flüsse unternehmen.

Im ersten Satz reden wir über Regierungen, Arbeitslosigkeit und Umweltverschmutzung im **Allgemeinen**. Deshalb lassen wir im Englischen den bestimmten Artikel weg.

Im zweiten Satz dagegen ist von **spezifischen** Regierungen, Arbeitslosigkeit einer bestimmten Gruppe und Umweltverschmutzung eines Gebietes die Rede.

→ Der bestimmte Artikel wird in den folgenden Einzelfällen **nicht** verwendet:
vor **most** ❸, vor Straßennamen ❹, mit Körperteilen ❺ – bei Körperteilen benutzen wir in der Regel ein Possessivpronomen (**my**, **his**, **her** usw.)

Exercise 4 Use **the** only when necessary. When the article is not required, put an **x** into the space.

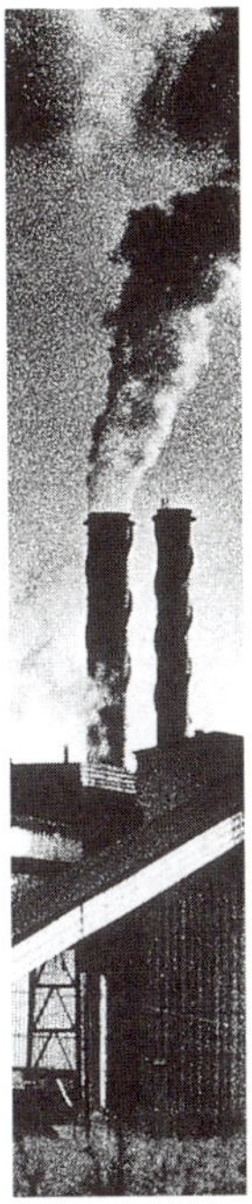

1 One of ______ biggest problems facing ______ mankind is ______ destruction of ______ natural environment by ______ industrial pollution.

2 At ______ world environmental summit in 1993 ______ Brazilian economics minister pointed out that ______ starving poor of Africa and Latin America can only be helped by ______ fast economic growth.

3 "It is easy for ______ rich to talk about saving ______ Amazonian rain forests and setting up ______ nature reserves for ______ tigers and ______ elephants," ______ minister said, "but what about ______ poor? Do they not have ______ same right to ______ food, ______ shelter and ______ education as ______ peoples of ______ northern hemisphere?"

Exercise 5 Finish translating the sentences into English.

Alcoholism is a growing problem.

der Alkoholismus

1 ______________ still has a great influence ________________ .

die Religion; auf die Gesellschaft.

2 A lot of Scots want ____________________ from England.

die Unabhängigkeit

3 ________________________________ still feel disadvantaged.

die meisten Minderheiten

4 Until recently South Wales was dependent ________________ .

von dem Kohlenbergbau

5 If _______________ are not willing to protect ____________ we will all die out. *Regierungen; die Natur*

6 In most EU countries ____________ must go to ____________ until they are 16. *Kinder; die Schule*

A 4 Grundfehler mit dem Genitiv

① The ~~car's door~~ was damaged in the accident.
② The ~~poor's situation~~ is getting worse, not better.
③ ~~Charles'~~ flat is very expensive.

✓ ❶ **The door of the car** was damaged in the accident.
✓ ❷ **The situation of the poor** is getting worse, not better.
✓ ❸ Charle**s's** flat is very expensive.

→ Die Grundregel lautet:
of-Genitiv bei **Sachen** ❶ und bei **Adjektiven**, die als Substantive gebraucht werden ❷.
's-Genitiv bei **Menschen** ❸, **Tieren** sowie bei **Zeitausdrücken** wie z.B. **last week** / **month** / **year**, **yesterday**, **today**, **tomorrow** und **next week** / **month** / … .

→ Der **'s**-Genitiv wird wie folgt gebildet:

Singular:	the girl**'s** cat, the woman**'s** job, Jame**s's** room
Plural:	the girl**s'** cat, the Brown**s'** house, the Davi**s's** son
	the childre**n's** room, the me**n's** jobs

→ Beachten Sie diese Besonderheiten:
Jill and Jane**'s** cars *(die Autos gehören Jill und Jane gemeinsam)*
Sarah**'s** and Jane**'s** cars *(Sarah und Jane besitzen jeweils ein Auto)*

This is a photo **of my son's**. *(das Foto gehört dem Sohn)*
This is a photo **of my son**. *(das Foto zeigt den Sohn)*

Exercise 1 Use the correct form of the **'s**-genitive.

1 ______________________________ looks like a rubbish tip.
→ *the Harpers + garden*

2 Have you met ______________________________ before?
→ *Gladys + husband*

3 The ______________________________ were over 2000 words long.
→ *students + essays*

4 You shouldn't borrow ____________________ without asking her.
→ *Mrs Adams + bike*

5 This room used to be ______________________________ .
→ *the children + playroom*

Exercise 2 Use the correct form of the genitive.

1 When the firemen arrived, ______________________________ was already burning. *the roof + the house*

2 Columbus never realized that ______________________________ would change ______________________________ .
the discovery + America; the course + human history

3 Jake took ______________________________ without permission.
his dad + car

4 Mrs Jackson is the ______________________________ .
She's also ______________________________ .
head teacher + our school; Charles + mother

5 H. G. Wells said that in ______________________________ the one-eyed is king. *the land + the blind*

6 In the 19th century ______________________________ often built their villas near ______________________________ .
the owners + factories; the entrance + the works

7 Caroline is fanatical about ______________________________ .
She calls people who eat frogs' legs "______________________".
animals + rights; the assassins + nature

8 There can be no doubt that ______________________________ depends on ______________________________ .
future + Europe; success + EU

9 Have you seen ______________________________ ?
Channel 4 is broadcasting ______________________________ .
tonight + TV guide; Jane + new play

10 I can't stand people who push their way to ______________________________ . *the front + the queue*

A 5 Grundfehler mit Substantiven

1 Schwierigkeiten mit dem Plural

① Can I have ~~two breads~~, please?
② The police ~~is~~ stopping all traffic from leaving the town.
③ Have you got ~~a scissors~~, please? – Yes, here it is.

✓ ❶ Can I have two **loaves of bread**, please?
✓ ❷ The police **are** stopping all traffic from leaving the town.
✓ ❸ Have you got **some** / **a pair of** scissors, please? – Yes, here **they are**.

→ Generell ist für Deutsche die englische Pluralbildung kein großes Problem. Es gibt jedoch vier Fehlerquellen, die sogar in der Oberstufe immer wieder auftreten, und zwar:
- die Missachtung der Schreibregeln,
- die Tendenz, im Englischen nichtzählbare Substantive im Plural zu benutzen ❶,
- die gelegentliche Missachtung von unregelmäßigen Formen,
- der Gebrauch von Substantiven ohne Singularform ❷, ❸.

→ Mit wenigen Ausnahmen bilden wir die **Pluralform** durch das Anhängen eines -(e)s. Beachten Sie aber die Schreibregeln:

Endet der Singular auf -ch, -sh, -ss oder -x, wird der Plural mit -es gebildet: **switch** – switch**es**, **wish** – wish**es**, **glass** – glass**es**, **fox** – fox**es**

Endet der Singular auf **Konsonant +** -y, bilden wir den Plural auf -ies: **city** – cit**ies**, **family** – famil**ies**, **lorry** – lorr**ies**

Endet der Singular auf -o, wird der Plural meist auf -oes gebildet: **echo** – ech**oes**, **embargo** – embarg**oes**, **ghetto** – ghett**oes**, **hero** – her**oes**
Beachten Sie aber: **disco** – disc**os**, **kilo** – kil**os**, **photo** – phot**os**

Endet der Singular auf -f bzw. -fe – nicht aber auf -ff –, bilden wir den Plural meist auf -ves: **knife** – kni**ves**, **life** – li**ves**, **scarf** – scar**ves**, **shelf** – shel**ves**
Beachten Sie aber: **belief** – belie**fs**, **chief** – chie**fs**, **handkerchief** – handkerchie**fs**

→ **Nichtzählbare Substantive** haben keine Pluralform. Sie können also nicht mit **Zahlen**, mit **Ausdrücken der unbestimmten Menge** (**a number of**, **many** und **several**) oder mit **a** / **an** verwendet werden ❶. Wollen wir ein nichtzählbares Substantiv im Plural verwenden, dann müssen wir einen geeigneten zählbaren Ausdruck hinzufügen (siehe Seite 27).

a / an	aerosol	of	paint, perfume, …	*eine Spraydose Lack, Parfüm, …*
	bag		crisps, sweets, …	*eine Tüte Chips, Süßigkeiten, …*
	bar		chocolate, soap, …	*eine Tafel Schokolade, ein Stück Seife, …*
	bottle		beer, milk, …	*eine Flasche Bier, Milch, …*
	box		chocolates, …	*eine Schachtel Pralinen, …*
	can		beer, paint, …	*eine Dose Bier, Farbe, …*
	crate		mineral water, …	*ein Kasten Mineralwasser, …*
	glass		fruit juice, wine, …	*ein Glas Fruchtsaft, Wein, …*
	jar		honey, jam, …	*ein Glas Honig, Marmelade, …*
	litre		petrol, wine, …	*ein Liter Benzin, Wein, …*
	loaf		bread	*ein Laib Brot*
	piece		cheese, ham, …	*ein Stück Käse, Schinken, …*
	pound		butter, cheese, …	*ein Pfund Butter, Käse, …*
	slice		bread, meat, …	*eine Scheibe Brot, Fleisch, …*
	tin		peas, soup, …	*eine Dose Erbsen, Suppe, …*

→ Einige wenige Substantive haben eine **unregelmäßige Pluralform**, die man sich einfach merken muss:
child – child**ren, man** – men, **woman** – women, **foot** – feet, **goose** – geese, **tooth** – teeth, **mouse** – mice

→ Der **endungslose Plural**:
Nationalitäten auf -**ese:** a **Chinese** – two Chin**ese**, a **Portuguese** – a number of Portugu**ese**

Transportmittel auf -**craft:** an **aircraft** – four air**craft**, a **hovercraft** – a lot of hover**craft**, a **spacecraft** – three space**craft**

Verschiedenes:
a **deer** – two deer, a **fish** – three fish, a **sheep** – several sheep, a **series** – four series, a **Swiss** – six Swiss

→ Die drei wichtigen Wörter **people**, **police** und **youth** haben keine Singularform und werden immer im Plural gebraucht:
People are angry about taxation. **They want** a change of government.
Many conservatives think **the police are** not paid enough.
The **youth** of today **are** worried about **their** future.

Wollen wir diese Wörter im Singular benutzen, müssen wir **person** (statt *people*), **policeman** / -**woman** (statt *police*) bzw. **young man** / **woman** / **person** (statt *youth*) verwenden:
John **is a person** who has problems making friends.
There **is** always **a policeman** outside 10 Downing Street.
A young woman helped me find the station.

Beachten Sie aber:
Some **people** are really funny.
Einige Menschen sind wirklich komisch.
There are many different **peoples** in Russia.
Es gibt viele verschiedene Völker in Russland.
I think modern **youth** have a lot of problems.
Ich meine, dass die moderne Jugend viele Probleme hat.
I saw **a youth** talking to an old lady.
Ich sah einen jungen Mann, der mit einer alten Dame sprach.

→ Werkzeuge und Kleidung, die aus zwei miteinander verbundenen Teilen bestehen, sind immer Plural und unzählbar.
Am wichtigsten sind **tin cutters** *(Blechschneider)*, **pliers** *(Zange)*, **scissors** *(Schere)*, **tweezers** *(Pinzette)*, **jeans**, **pants** *(Unterhose)*, **pyjamas**, **shorts**, **trousers**:
These tweezers are for picking up small objects.
The **red shorts were** more expensive than the **green ones**.

Wollen wir Wörter dieser Gruppe im Singular benutzen, fügen wir **a pair of** *(ein Paar)* hinzu:
I'd like **a pair of trousers**, please.
Ich hätte gerne eine Hose, bitte.
Have you got **a pair of cutters** suitable for hard steel?
Haben Sie ein Schneidewerkzeug, das für Hartstahl geeignet ist?

Exercise 1 Put the English equivalents of the German nouns into the sentences. Use plurals as necessary. Be careful about spelling.

1 Immigrant ____________ are in fact made up of countless ______________________ . ↝ *Gesellschaft*; *Minderheit*

2 The great ______________ of Norfolk show how rich the ____________ once was. ↝ *Kirche*; *Grafschaft*

3 The best ________________ of the ________________ of soldiers in the ________________ were written by the war poets. ↝ *Beschreibung*; *Leben*; *Schützengraben* [trench]

4 Neil Postman writes convincingly about ______________ and ____________ . ↝ *Fernsehen*; *Gesellschaft*

5 The patterns made by ____________ is one of this artist's favourite ____________ . ↝ *Dach*; *Motiv*

6 Lear and Othello are Shakespeare's most tragic ____________ . ↝ *Held*

Exercise 2 Use a word from the list to complete the sentences. Only one solution is possible.

aerosols, bar, bars, bottles, crates, gallons, tubs, tubes

1 No wonder Brenda's so fat. She ate three ________ chocolate last night.

2 You can't buy ________ petrol in the UK now, just litres.

3 In Germany ________ beer are largely standardized.

4 Isn't it ridiculous to sell ________ toothpaste in boxes?

5 Never buy ________ shaving cream. Use a brush and a ________ soap.

6 The big problem with ________ milk is their weight.

7 The big ________ ice-cream have six balls and the small ones four.

Exercise 3 Complete the sentences with the nouns in italics. Use singular or plural forms as necessary.

1 There was so much ________ lying around that it had attracted ________ and ________ . *food; mouse; fly*

2 A lot of ________ are against the ________ of ________ to make paté.

animal lover; forced feeding; goose

3 ________ say that ________ are destroying the ________ of generations of ________.

dentist; sweet; tooth; child

4 We just have to accept that there are a few ________ that are done best by ________ – drilling for ________ , for example. *job; man; oil*

5 There are no less than six ________ of these awful ________ on TV at the moment. *series; soap opera*

6 The big ________ with ________ is that they are nearly as noisy as ________ .
Most ________ prefer to travel by ________ .

problem; hovercraft; aircraft; passenger; ship

Exercise 4 Translate the sentences into English.

1 *Meiner Meinung nach ist die deutsche Jugend viel besser als ihr Ruf.*

In my opinion ______________________________________

than its reputation.

2 *Vergiss nicht, einen Schlafanzug mitzubringen.*

Don't forget to bring ____________________________ with you.

3 *Geschäftsleute müssen lernen, dass Menschen steigende Preise nicht akzeptieren werden.*

_____________________ must learn that _________________

__________________ rising prices.

4 *Ein Polizist hat drei junge Männer angehalten.*

__________________ stopped _________________________ .

5 *Wir brauchen eine Zange, um dieses Teil herauszunehmen.*

We need _____________________________________ this part.

6 *Die Völker der Sahara gehören zu den ärmsten der Welt.*

_______________________________ are among ___________

____________________________ .

2 Knifflige nichtzählbare Substantive

① There ~~are~~ some more ~~informations~~ at the back of the book.
② ~~Furnitures are~~ nearly 50% cheaper in the sale.
③ The ~~news are bad~~, I'm afraid.

✓ ❶ There **is** some more **information** at the back of the book.
✓ ❷ **Furniture is** nearly 50% cheaper in the sale.
✓ ❸ The news **is** bad, I'm afraid.

→ Beachten Sie, dass im Englischen einige wichtige Wörter wie **advice**, **evidence**, **furniture**, **information**, **news**, **progress** und **research** **unzählbar** sind. Deshalb steht das Verb immer im **Singular** ❶, ❷, ❸.

→ Möchten wir diese Wörter **im Plural benutzen**, können wir – mit Ausnahme von *progress* – **a piece of** … bzw. **a bit of** … hinzufügen: You will find **several pieces / bits of evidence** for this argument in the text.

We've had two **pieces / bits of news** today.
Wendy has done **several pieces / bits of research** into how children learn.

→ Merken Sie sich, dass bei **progress** nur **a bit of** … verwendet wird:
Poor Tom has only made **a bit of progress** since his operation.

Exercise 5 Use the correct form of the noun in italics. Use **a piece of** where necessary.

1 If you need any more ____________________ , just give us a ring.
information

2 I've just had some fantastic ______________ – I've won the lottery.
news

3 A lot of young people buy their ____________________ on credit.
furniture

4 We found two beautiful ________________________ at the auction.
furniture

5 You should have mentioned the three important ______________ ________________ on page two. *evidence*

6 This report is about an interesting __________________________ into alternative energy. *research*

Exercise 6 Spot and correct the mistake. There is one mistake in each sentence.

1 I read somewhere that grey wolfs are returning to western Europe.
2 The police is interviewing everybody in the road.
3 You can't risk human lifes to save animals.
4 You know what they say: No news are good news.
5 A lot of aircrafts are late in the holiday season.
6 We needed five litres of white paints to cover that awful purple wall.
7 Hand me a pliers, please.
8 Sitting Bull was one of the bravest Sioux chieves.

A 6 Grundfehler mit Pronomen

1 Self-Pronomen und *each other / one another*

① I won't be a moment. I'm just shaving ~~myself~~.
② We ~~enjoyed us~~ a lot at the party.
③ Tom and Sarah love ~~themselves~~.

✓ ❶ I won't be a moment. I'm just **shaving**.
✓ ❷ We **enjoyed ourselves** a lot at the party.
✓ ❸ Tom and Sarah love **each other / one another**.

→ Im Englischen benutzen wir **self**-Pronomen als **rückbezügliche** – oder reflexive – **Pronomen** *(reflexive pronouns)* ❷ und als **betonende Pronomen** *(emphasizing pronouns).*

→ Im Gegensatz zum Deutschen gibt es im Englischen nur eine kleine Zahl von Verben, die reflexiv gebraucht wird. Am wichtigsten sind:

amuse	You can always **amuse yourself** in a big city. *Man kann sich in einer Großstadt immer gut amüsieren.*
cut	Be careful. You might **cut yourself**. *Sei vorsichtig! Du könntest dich schneiden.*
defend	You should **defend yourself** against unfair criticism. *Sie sollten sich gegen unfaire Kritik verteidigen.*
enjoy	I didn't **enjoy myself** in London at all. *Ich habe mich in London überhaupt nicht gut unterhalten.*
help	It's a buffet. We can **help ourselves**. *Es ist ein Buffet. Wir können uns (selbst) bedienen.*
hurt	Bob **hurt himself** with a knife. *Bob hat sich mit einem Messer verletzt.*
introduce	The speaker **introduced herself** as Dr Mary Green. *Die Rednerin stellte sich als Dr. Mary Green vor.*
look after	They are too ill to **look after themselves**. *Sie sind zu krank, um sich selbst zu versorgen.*

→ Beachten Sie insbesondere diese Verben, die im Englischen **ohne ein self**-Pronomen gebraucht werden:

sich ändern – **change**
sich beschweren – **complain**
sich beziehen auf – **refer to**
sich entschuldigen – **apologize**
sich erinnern – **remember**
sich hinlegen – **lie down**
sich öffnen – **open**
sich schließen – **close**
sich streiten – **argue**
sich verstecken – **hide**
sich waschen – **wash**
sich beeilen – **hurry**
sich bewegen – **move**
sich empfehlen – **recommend**
sich entspannen – **relax**
sich fühlen – **feel**
sich merken – **remember, note**
sich rasieren – **shave**
sich setzen – **sit down**
sich treffen – **meet**
sich etwas vorstellen – **imagine**
sich wünschen – **wish for**

→ Bei den deutschen Reflexivverben gibt es nur in der 3. Person eine besondere Form: (er / sie) sich. Bei den anderen Personen sind Reflexivpronomen und Personalpronomen identisch: (ich) mich, (du) dich, (wir) uns usw. Diese Erscheinung führt dazu, dass Schüler gelegentlich ein Personalpronomen *(me, your, us)* statt eines der **self**-Pronomen benutzen.
Beachten Sie die Schreibweise der 3. Person Singular und der Pluralformen.

I	**my**self	we	**our**sel**ves**
you	**your**self	you	**your**sel**ves**
he / she / it	**him**self / **her**self / **it**self	they	**them**sel**ves**

→ Wenn eine Handlung auf Gegenseitigkeit beruht, verwenden wir im Englischen **kein self-Pronomen**, sondern **each other** / **one another** (einander). Vergleichen Sie:
The Greens are so boastful. They really **love themselves**.
Die Greens sind so angeberisch. Sie sind wirklich in sich verliebt.
John and Mary **love each other** and want to get married.
John und Mary lieben sich (gegenseitig) und möchten heiraten.

→ **Merken** Sie sich, dass **each other** und **one another** dieselbe Bedeutung und die gleiche Form für alle Personen haben.

Exercise 1 Read the sentences. Fill in a **self**-pronoun or an object pronoun (**me**, **you**, **her**, ...).

1 When I saw the old lady fall, I thought to myself ______ that she would never get up again.

2 I couldn't see a yard in front of me ______ in the fog and I kept hearing footsteps behind me ______ .

3 In a test always ask ______________ this question: "What does the examiner expect _________ to tell _________ ".

4 I'm sorry. We can't cook for you ______ . You'll have to get your meals yourself ______ .

5 Frank Bond is so selfish. He is only only interested in himself ______ . But what about his family? He never thinks of them ______ .

6 The English for *Baumarkt* is often "Do-it-yourself ______ Store".

7 When Anne gets back from work she likes to have half an hour just to ______________ . She can't stand it when people keep talking to _________ .

Exercise 2 Read the sentences. Say if the **self**-pronouns are used emphatically (**e**) or reflexively (**r**). (If you can take the **self**-pronoun out without destroying the sentence, it has been used emphatically.)

1 I like that table. Did you make it yourself? ( )

2 The film was great. We enjoyed ourselves a lot. ( )

3 Tom cut himself opening a can of peas. ( )

4 I can't remember anything about the incident myself. ( )

5 I'm sorry, but I've got to go.
You'll have to finish the job yourself. ( )

6 May I introduce myself? My name's David Clarke. ( )

Exercise 3 Put in the correct form of the **self**-pronouns.

1 Ann loves TV but I can't stand it ____________ .

2 The party was awful. Nobody seemed to enjoy ____________ much.

3 You two are so noisy. Why can't you behave ____________ ?

4 Sarah painted this picture ____________ .

5 The bird hurt ____________ when it flew into a closed window.

6 My new boss introduced ____________ as "Professor Dr Dr Hartmann".

Exercise 4 Fill in the English equivalents of the German verbs. Use the tenses or forms given in italic. Put in **self**-pronouns only where necessary.

1 What has happened to Claire? She ____________ beyond all recognition. ↝ *present perfect: sich ändern*

2 Are you all right? Don't you think you should ____________ ?
↝ *simple present: sich hinsetzen sollen*

3 At the beginning of the lecture the speaker ____________ ____________ to the audience. ↝ *simple past: sich vorstellen*

4 Unfortunately, most children ____________ mainly by watching TV. ↝ *simple present: sich amüsieren*

5 Look out! You ____________ if you're not careful.
↝ *will-future: sich verletzen*

6 How can the government expect the mentally ill ________________ ________________ ? *infinitive: sich selbst versorgen*

7 There's no need to order drinks. We can ________________ from the mini-bar. *simple present: sich selbst bedienen können*

8 Please ________________ that we are closed on Mondays until Easter. *imperative: sich merken*

Exercise 5 Complete the sentences with a **self**-pronoun or **each other**.

1 Alison always looks at ________________ as she walks past shop windows.

2 Only marry if you really want to live with ________________ for the rest of your lives.

3 Have you fed the dog? You can't expect her to get her food ________________ , you know.

4 I can't understand boxing. What's the fun in two men hitting ________________ ?

5 It's nonsense to claim that people who talk to ________________ are mad. Psychologists say that a lot of us talk to ________________ more than to ________________ .

6 You don't need to write. We'll see ________________ at Tom's party next week.

7 Frank should see ________________ as others see him – then he wouldn't make such a fool of ________________ all the time.

8 The whole idea of working with a partner is that you help ________________ ________________ . That's much more important than working just for ________________ .

2 Die Demonstrativpronomen *this / that, these / those*

① ~~This texts~~ here are quite difficult.
② Look at ~~these~~ boys over there.

✓ ❶ **These texts** here are quite difficult.
✓ ❷ Look at **those boys** over there.

these texts

those boys

→ Die Hauptfehlerquellen bei den Demonstrativpronomen sind: der Gebrauch von **this** statt **these** ❶ und der Gebrauch von **this** / **these** *(diese/-r/-s)* statt **that** / **those** *(jene/-r/-s)* ❷.

→ Räumlich benutzen wir **this** / **these** bei Personen, Sachen usw., die nah beieinander sind, und **that** / **those** bei Personen, Sachen usw., die weiter entfernt sind.

→ Zeitlich werden **this** / **these**, **that** / **those** genauso verwendet.
Vergleichen Sie:

Gegenwart:	The world **is** changing very fast **these days**. *Heutzutage ändert sich die Welt sehr schnell.*
Vergangenheit:	He **was** much happier in **those** days. *Er war viel glücklicher zu jener Zeit.*

Exercise 6 Put in the missing demonstrative pronouns.

1 She picked up the book and said, "Who does ________ belong to?"

2 You can't interpret Luther without understanding life in ___________ days.

3 I first met Harry in 1985. At ___________ time he was teaching in London.

4 Helen looked across the room. "___________ woman in red is Vanessa Redgrave", she said.

5 Of course I am worried about the future in ___________ days of high unemployment.

6 Look at ___________ advertisement here. ___________ house we saw yestersay is for sale.

A 7 Grundfehler bei Bezeichnungen für unbestimmte Mengen

1 *some / any* und ihre Zusammensetzungen

① I haven't got ~~some~~ money.
② Have you read ~~something~~ about the disaster?
③ Can I have ~~any~~ coffee, please?

✓ ❶ I haven't got **any** money.
✓ ❷ Have you read **anything** about the disaster?
✓ ❸ Can I have **some** coffee, please?

→ Die Bedeutung von **some** und **any** *(einige/-r/-s, etwas, irgendein/-e)* ist identisch, aber die beiden Wörter werden unterschiedlich gebraucht. Wie bei vielen Fehlern, liegt die Schwierigkeit darin, dass es im Deutschen diesen Unterschied nicht gibt.

→ Ob wir **some** or **any** benutzen, hat im Grunde mit **Gewissheit** zu tun. Will der Sprecher behaupten, dass irgendetwas sicherlich existiert, bzw. so ist, dann benutzt er **some**. Möchte er aber die Existenz von irgendetwas verneinen, bzw. in Frage stellen, benutzt er **any**.
Aus diesem Grund verwenden wir logischerweise
some in **bejahten Aussagen** und
any in **verneinten Aussagen** und **Fragen ❶, ❷**.

Vergleichen Sie diese Sätze:
We are reading **some** texts about minorities at the moment.
Not all minorities are discriminated against; **some** are very privileged.
We haven't read **any** fictional texts about minorities yet.
Have you got **any** texts about discrimination at work?

→ Wir benutzen die Zusammensetzungen **somebody** / **anybody**, **someone** / **anyone**, **something** / **anything**, und **somewhere** / **anywhere** in genau derselben Art und Weise:
Somebody said that children are a minority, too.
I can't find out **anything** about the Innuit.
Have you seen my dictionary **anywhere**?

→ Bei höflichen **Bitten** in der **Frageform,** die keine echten informationssuchenden Fragen sind, benutzen wir logischerweise **some ❸**.

Exercise 1 Complete the dialogues with **some** or **any.**

1 "Have we got __________ wine? I'd like __________ if we have."

"Sorry. I wanted to buy __________ but they didn't have __________ of the wine you like. Have __________ beer instead."

2 "I couldn't get __________ stamps because I didn't have __________ money with me. It's a real nuisance – I've got __________ important letters to send off."

"Why don't you ask Mrs Brown if she's got __________ stamps? She usually has __________ in the house."

3 "Can you find __________ time to talk about the Sheffield project this morning? We can't put off a decision __________ longer."

"You're right. How about 10.30? I haven't got __________ appointments then."

Exercise 2 Complete the dialogues with **some, any** or one of their compounds.

1 "Has ________________ seen Sally? I can't find her ________________ ."

"Well, I'm not sure but I think I heard her saying ________________ to ________________ about going home early."

2 "I'm sure you'd like ________________ to eat before you leave. There's ________________ ham in the fridge. I could make ________________ sandwiches."

"Thanks a lot. You never get ________________ to eat at the Snows'."

3 "Are you doing ________________ important at the moment, Wendy? If not, I need ________________ help with these statistics."

"Okay then, but I've got to go ________________ at 3 o'clock. You'll have to ask ________________ else to help you then."

2 *much / many / a lot of (lots of), plenty of*

① Jill has got ~~many~~ books.
② Tom earns ~~much~~ money as a computer salesman.
③ We've got ~~very much~~ bread. Don't buy any.

✓ ❶ Jill has got **a lot of / lots of books**.
✓ ❷ Tom earns **a lot of / lots of money** as a computer salesman.
✓ ❸ We've got **plenty of bread**. Don't buy any.

→ Wie bei **some** / **any** haben auch **much** / **many** / **a lot of** dieselbe Bedeutung. Man muss daher auf ihren **Gebrauch** achten.

→ Wir benutzen **many** mit zählbaren und **much** mit nichtzählbaren Substantiven in **verneinten Aussagen** und **Fragen**:
I couldn't buy **many steaks** because I didn't have **much money** with me.
Does your teacher show **much interest** in your work?

In **bejahten Aussagen** benutzen wir **a lot of** / **lots of** mit **zählbaren** sowie **nichtzählbaren** Substantiven ❶, ❷:
Minorities are protected by law in **a lot of** / **lots of countries**.
A lot of / **Lots of water** is polluted by farm chemicals.

→ Möchten wir „mehr als genug" ausdrücken, verwenden wir **plenty of** mit **zählbaren** sowie **nichtzählbaren** Substantiven ❸:
There's **plenty of beer** in the fridge. Just help yourself.
Why did you buy so much bread? We've got **plenty of rolls**.

→ Beachten Sie, dass wir **a lot of** / **lots of** nach **as**, **so**, **too**, **how** und **very** nicht verwenden können:
Come on. We haven't got **very much time**.
Aletha's a nice girl, but she talks **too much**.
We didn't score **as many points** as the other team.

Exercise 3 Translate the sentences into English. Use **much, many** or **a lot of**.

1 *Wir haben viele Mädchen in unserer Gruppe, aber nicht viele Jungen.*

We have got ______________________________ in our group, but

______________________________ .

2 *Beeil Dich! Wir haben nicht viel Zeit.*

Hurry up! We haven't got ________________________ .

3 *Wie viel Geld soll ich holen? Wir werden viel (Geld) am Wochenende brauchen.*

_______________ should I get? We'll need _______ _______________ .

4 *Sie rauchen zuviel, Herr Snow – und Sie sollten auch nicht so viel arbeiten.*

You _______________, Mr Snow – and _______________, either.

Exercise 4 Complete the sentences with **much**, **many**, **a lot of** or **plenty of**.

1 _______ doctors say that we use too _______ salt in our food.

2 We needn't stop at the filling-station. There's _______ petrol in the car already and we won't need _______ to get to Southport and back.

3 The textile industry employs _______ women, but they don't earn _______ money. They don't have _______ chance of promotion, either.

4 It's easy enough to find _______ reasons not to do something but you won't make _______ money that way.

5 There isn't _______ evidence that minorities benefit from the _______ laws that have been introduced to protect them. There is as _______ prejudice as there ever was.

6 _______ industrialists think that jobs in Germany cost too _______ . They point out that even within the EU _______ their competitors have too _______ of an advantage.

7 Why on earth are you running? We've got _______ time before the train leaves.

3 a few / a little, few / little

① We only met ~~few tourists~~.
② Tricia has ~~few enthusiasm~~ for her work.

❶ We only met **a few tourists.**
❷ Tricia has **little enthusiasm** for her work.

→ **A few** heißt „ein paar", **a little** bedeutet „ein wenig".
Ohne Artikel bedeutet **few** „wenige" und **little** „wenig".

→ Wir benutzen (a) **few** mit **zählbaren** ❶ und (a) **little** mit **nichtzählbaren** Substantiven ❷.

Dies gilt für alle Satzarten:

Don't forget to buy **a few tomatoes**.	*ein paar*
Would you like **a little sugar**?	*ein wenig*
Few people are as helpful as Joan.	*wenige*
A lot of pupils have **little time** for school.	*wenig*

Exercise 5 Fill in (a) **little**, (a) **few**.

1 Unfortunately a lot of businessmen have __________ time for their families.

2 __________ ordinary supermarkets sell caviar. They say there's __________ demand for it.

3 We've only got __________ dollars left so you had better pay with a credit card.

4 Very __________ people are willing to give __________ of their time to charity. Most people prefer to put __________ coins in a box.

5 Stop shouting. Why can't you show __________ more patience?

6 __________ criminals are impressed by the threat of punishment because there is __________ chance of them being caught.

7 The recipe says you should add __________ fresh lemon juice to the chicken sauce.

Exercise 6 Read the situations and say which expression of indefinite quantity you would use in each. Only one solution is possible.

Sie möchten jemandem sagen, dass ...

1 ... *Sie reichlich Essen haben.*

____

2 ... *viele Frauen sich immer noch benachteiligt fühlen.*

____

3 ... *wenige Politiker staatsmännisch denken können.*

____

4 ... *nur ein wenig Fleisch übrig geblieben ist.*

____

5 ... *Sie nicht sehr viel Zeit haben.*

(not) _______________

6 ... *Sie nicht viele Eintrittskarten verkauft haben.*

(not) _______________

7 ... *Sie einige Briefmarken ausleihen möchten.*

____

8 ... *Sie gerne ein paar Tomaten hätten.*

____

9 ... *es wenig Zweck hat, Tiere im Nachhinein zu bestrafen.*

____

10 ... *Sie kein Bargeld bei sich haben.*

____

11 ... *Sie keine Lust haben, noch ein Video anzusehen.*

____

12 ... *wenig Menschen bereit sind, mehr für die Umwelt zu tun.*

____

13 ... *Sie gern einige Informationen über den Kurs hätten.*

____

A 8 Grundfehler mit modalen Hilfsverben

1 Form

① I ~~must to run~~ or I'll miss my bus.
② Tom ~~doesn't can play~~ chess.
③ We ~~will must~~ do our homework before breakfast.

✓ ❶ I **must run** or I'll miss my bus.
✓ ❷ Tom **can't / cannot play** chess.
✓ ❸ We **will have to do** our homework before breakfast.

→ Generell sind die modalen Hilfsverben für Deutschsprachige kein großes Problem. Wegen der aber teilweise starken optischen Ähnlichkeit zwischen Deutsch und Englisch schleichen sich oft Fehler ein.

→ Im Englischen werden modale Hilfsverben nur in Verbindung mit einem Vollverb gebraucht. Das Vollverb steht im Infinitiv **ohne** *to*. Alle Personen zeigen dieselbe Form – die 3. Person Singular hat also **keine** *-s*-Endung. Bei allen Hilfsverben wird die Verneinung und die Fragestellung wie im Deutschen – das heißt **ohne** *do* – gebildet ❶, ❷:
We **must work** harder.
Sally **cannot come** to the party tonight.
Drivers **should not go** too fast near schools.
Can we smoke in here?
May I open the window?
Shall we go to the cinema?

→ Anders als im Deutschen haben die englischen modalen Hilfsverben keinen Infinitiv und können nicht alle Zeitformen bilden. Möchten wir die fehlenden Zeiten gebrauchen, benutzen wir **Ersatzverben** mit ähnlicher Bedeutung.

→ Ersatzverb **have to** für **must**:
John **had to go** to New York on business last week.
I **haven't had to see** a doctor for years.
Wendy **will have to write** the letters tomorrow.

→ Ersatzverb **be able to** für **can** / **could** (Fähigkeit):
Tom **has been able to speak** German since he was a little boy.
The doctor says I **will be able to lead** a normal life again after my operation.

→ Ersatzverb **be allowed to** für **can** / **could** (Erlaubnis):
Sandra's dad is strict. She **has never been allowed to go out** alone.
Do you think we **will be allowed to stay up** late at the weekend?

Exercise 1 Complete the sentences with the English equivalents of the German expressions.

☀ You **can see** Mr Gregg at three. ⇝ *sehen können*

1 The Browns ______________ more polite to their neighbours.

⇝ *sein sollten*

2 ______________________________ your car at the weekend?

⇝ *ich + ausleihen dürfen*

3 ______________________________ the children from school today?

⇝ *wir + abholen sollen*

4 Tourists ______________________________ church services.

⇝ *nicht stören sollten*

5 I've got toothache. I ______________ to the dentist's.

⇝ *hingehen müssen*

6 The boss said we ____________________ a day off on Friday.

⇝ *haben können*

Exercise 2 Complete the sentences with the English equivalent of **müssen.** Use the tense given. Be careful about questions.

1 We ____________ get up very early. Our plane leaves at 6.30 am.

⇝ *present*

2 It's terrible. I ____________ wait over two hours to see the doctor.

⇝ *past*

3 ____________________ (I) stay in hospital long?

⇝ *will-future*

4 Ben ______________ walk to work since he lost his driving licence.

⇝ *present perfect*

5 Tom ____________ do overtime every day this week.

⇝ *present*

6 Our TV's broken. We __________________________ buy a new one.

⇝ *going to-future*

Exercise 3 Complete the sentences with the equivalent of **können** using the tenses and functions given. Be careful about questions.

1 My boss says I ______________ have a holiday before June.

→ *simple present: Erlaubnis + nicht*

2 Betty ____________________________ leave her bed for a week.

→ *present perfect: Fähigkeit + nicht*

3 Do you think we ____________________________ visit the Kremlin?

→ *will-future: Erlaubnis*

4 ____________________________ they help the people in the house?

→ *simple past: Fähigkeit*

5 ______________ you be here by 10 at the latest?

→ *simple present: Fähigkeit*

6 Harry ______________ help me with the report because he was busy. → *simple past: Möglichkeit + nicht*

2 Gebrauch

① Must I eat this curry? Of course not. You ~~mustn't~~ if you don't want to.
② Look at the sky. It ~~can~~ rain later.
③ ~~Will~~ we meet in the café?

✓ ❶ Must I eat this curry? Of course not. You **needn't / don't have to** if you don't want to.
✓ ❷ Look at the sky. It **could rain** later.
✓ ❸ **Shall we meet** in the café?

→ Beachten Sie, dass **must** – wie das deutsche Hilfsverb „müssen" – einen Zwang bzw. eine zwingende Notwendigkeit ausdrückt ❶:

Zwang:	You **must show** your passport at Dover. *Sie müssen Ihren Pass in Dover zeigen.*
Notwendigkeit:	Tom **must smoke** less or he will be ill. *Tom muss weniger rauchen oder er wird krank.*

→ Häufig stellt **mustn't** ein Problem dar. Die deutsche Entsprechung für **mustn't** ist nämlich „nicht dürfen". Es drückt also ein Verbot aus:
You **mustn't disturb** lessons.
Du darfst den Unterricht nicht stören.
We **mustn't open** the letter before tomorrow.
Wir dürfen den Brief nicht vor morgen öffnen.

→ Die englische Entsprechung für das deutsche Hilfsverb „nicht müssen" lautet **needn't** bzw. – als Ersatzverb – **not have to** ❶:

keine Notwendigkeit: I **needn't cut** / **don't have to cut** the lawn today. *Ich muss heute nicht / brauche heute nicht den Rasen zu mähen.*

kein Zwang: You **needn't work** / **don't have to work** late. *Du musst / brauchst nicht länger (zu) arbeiten.*

→ Im Englischen ist es nicht möglich, *can* zu benutzen, um eine Möglichkeit auszudrücken. Hier kommt nur **could** in Frage ❷:

Don't do that. It **could damage** the machine.

Tun Sie das nicht. Es könnte die Maschine beschädigen.

→ Es ist auch nicht möglich *Will I / we* … zu verwenden, um nach Vorschlägen zu fragen. In solchen Fällen benutzen wir immer **Shall** I / we … ❸.

Shall I make a cup of coffee? *Soll ich eine Tasse Kaffee machen?*

Shall we have a barbecue tomorrow? *Sollen wir morgen grillen?*

Exercise 4 Use **must, mustn't** or **needn't.**

☀ I **must** call in at the bank today. We need some cash.

1 You ____________ help me if you've got something else to do.

2 In most EU countries, people over 16 ____________ carry identity cards.

3 Ted ____________ answer all six questions, but he ____________ choose four.

4 You ____________ drive faster than 120 kph on Dutch motorways.

5 I hate restaurants where they tell you what you ____________ wear.

Exercise 5 Now rewrite the verbs in exercise 4 using a form of (**not**) **have to.** Mark the sentence where this is not possible with a cross (**x**).

☀ **have to** call in

1 ____________________ help

2 ____________________ carry

3 ____________________ answer, ____________________ choose

4 ____________________ drive

5 ____________________ wear

Exercise 6 Translate the parts in italics into German. Use infintive forms only.

☀ The British government's policy on Europe *will have to change* if the UK *does not want to become isolated*.

werden sich ändern müssen; nicht isoliert werden wollen.

1 Sarah *won't be able to come* to the party. She *must look after* her sick mother.

____

______________________________.

2 All doctors say that people *should not smoke* themselves but they *are unable to agree* on the question of 'passive smoking'.

____

______________________________.

3 *Can I have* the afternoon off tomorrow? I *would like to visit* my daughter's school.

____

______________________________.

4 You *mustn't drive* faster than 50 kph in towns but you *don't have to drive* so slowly on the open road.

____

______________________________.

5 A lot of British schoolchildren *needn't wear* uniforms nowadays. The schools *may decide* for themselves.

____

____

______________________________.

6 Look, we *ought to start* work. We *aren't allowed to go* home until we have finished.

____

____

______________________________.

A 9 Grundfehler bei der Stellung von Adverbien

① Sarah speaks ~~well~~ German.
② ~~Always~~ I am in bed by nine.
③ ~~Twice a week~~ I meet my friends.

✓ ❶ Sarah speaks German **well**.
✓ ❷ I am **always** in bed by nine.
✓ ❸ I meet my friends **twice a week**.

→ Anders als im Deutschen ist es im Englischen nicht möglich, ein Verb und sein Objekt durch ein Adverb zu trennen. Adverbien der **Art und Weise** *(adverbs of manner)* wie **beautifully**, **quickly**, **rudely**, **well** usw. stehen grundsätzlich **am Satzende** ❶:
The choir sang Mozart's *Requiem* **beautifully**.
The boss told us to finish the job **quickly**.
The policeman asked us for our papers **rudely**.

→ Bei Adverbien der Häufigkeit differenzieren wir zwischen Adverbien der **unbestimmten Häufigkeit** *(indefinite frequency)* wie **always**, **frequently**, **never**, **often**, **rarely**, **seldom**, **sometimes** usw. ❷ und Adverbien der **bestimmten Häufigkeit** *(definite frequency)* wie **annually**, **daily**, **every Monday**, **twice a week**, **yearly** usw. ❸.

Adverbien der **unbestimmten Häufigkeit** stellen wir in die Mitte des Satzes *(mid-position)* unmittelbar vor Vollverben und unmittelbar nach **be**:
Employers **often discriminate** against women.
You **can sometimes read** about racial prejudice in the press.
Tom **is always** late for work and he **is never** willing to do overtime.

Adverbien der **bestimmten Häufigkeit** dagegen stellen wir – wie auch Zeitadverbien – an das Satzende:
The Greens go to the cinema **twice a week**.
Carr & Co is growing faster **every year**.
Our newspaper is delivered **daily**.

→ Satzadverbien *(sentence adverbs)* wie **as a rule**, **generally speaking**, **luckily**, **naturally**, **of course**, **on the whole**, **perhaps**, **unfortunately**, die einen ganzen Satz bestimmen – stehen am Satzanfang.
In diesem Fall werden im Deutschen das Subjekt und das Verb ausgetauscht. Im Englischen dagegen **bleibt die Grundstellung unverändert**:

Adverb	Subjekt	Verb
Luckily,	**the ambulance**	**came** within a few minutes.

Die Einhaltung der Grundstellung gilt auch bei **there** + **be**:

As a rule,	**there are**	telephone boxes	at post offices.
Of course,	**there will be**	something to eat	at the party.

→ Da wir die meisten Adverbien an das Satzende stellen, gibt es oft mehrere Adverbien in dieser Position. In diesem Fall gilt die Reihenfolge:

	Art und Weise	Ort	Zeit
Sally Baker is ill. She can't come		**to work**	**tomorrow.**
Sally's doctor examined her	**thoroughly**		**an hour ago.**
She is now sitting	**nervously**	**in the waiting room.**	
Sally recovered	**quickly**	**in hospital**	**after her operation.**

Exercise 1 Use arrows to put the adverbs of frequency into the sentences.

1 Commentators claim that crime is caused by poverty. ~ *often*

2 Hard punishment leads to criminals changing their ways. ~ *seldom*

3 The number of tourists visiting Israel increases sharply. ~ *every Easter*

4 I have read such nonsense in my whole life. ~ *never*

5 Our English teacher shows us a video. ~ *now and then*

6 We are asked to prepare texts at home. ~ *usually*

Exercise 2 Use numbers to re-arrange the sentences in the correct order.

☀ every four years (**5**) is elected (**4**) of (**2**) the president (**1**) the USA (**3**)

1 because ( ) I didn't understand ( ) properly ( ) she didn't explain ( ) the problem ( )

2 can speak ( ) fluently ( ) Jenny Wood ( ) three languages ( )

3 always ( ) An eternal truth ( ) is ( ) is ( ) something ( ) that ( ) true ( )

4 achieve ( ) a solution ( ) can ( ) only ( ) politically ( ) We ( )

5 listened to ( ) The workers ( ) sceptically ( ) their employer's words ( ) very ( )

6 Always ( ) a new machine ( ) before ( ) carefully ( ) read ( ) switching on ( ) the instructions ( )

Exercise 3 Finish translating the sentences into English.

1 *Bald können wir gehen. Es hat fast aufgehört zu regnen.*

We ______________________________ . __________ almost stopped ______________ .

2 *Shakespeare wurde 1564 in Stratford geboren, aber er verbrachte die meiste Zeit seines Lebens in London.*

Shakespeare was born ___________________________ but he spent ______________________________________ .

3 *Leider muss ich am nächsten Wochenende arbeiten.*

____ .

4 *Vor 30 Jahren war es noch möglich, auf den Straßen ungefährdet zu spielen.*

It was _______________________ to play ________________

____ .

5 *Umfragen zeigen eindeutig, dass viele ältere Menschen Angst haben, ihre Wohnungen nachts zu verlassen.*

Surveys _________________ that a lot of older people _______

____ .

Exercise 4 Complete the table with adverbs from the list. In the case of adverbs in end-position, show their usual order, ie manner, place, definite frequency and time.

always, angrily, as a rule, at 10 am, at the party, each summer, every day, every other night, fast, in Berlin, in prison, last Christmas, luckily, noisily, of course, often, on the whole, out of bed, sadly, seldom, sometimes, today, twice a week

Front-	**Mid-**	**End-Position**		
		manner	*place*	*frequency / time*
	always			

A 10 Grundfehler beim Gebrauch der Simple und der Progressive Form

1 Nichtgebrauch der Progressive Form

① Sarah ~~is wanting~~ to buy a car.
② I ~~am liking~~ Jane more and more.

✓ ❶ Sarah **wants** to buy a car.
✓ ❷ I **like** Jane more and more.

→ Generall drückt die **Progressive Form** eine **andauernde** Handlung aus. Wir können also diese Form nur dann verwenden, wenn es sich um eine Tätigkeit mit zeitlicher Ausdehnung handelt:
Wendy **is cooking** and the children **are playing** in the garden.
We didn't go on holiday because we **were decorating** our flat.
Tom **has been working** on the report for more than a week.

→ Eine typische Fehlerquelle ist die Anwendung der Progressive Form bei Verben, die eine **sekundenschnelle Reaktion** oder **Empfindung** ausdrücken. Bei solchen Verben kommt das Progressive allein von der Logik her nie in Frage.
Die wichtigsten Verben sind:
assume *(annehmen)*, **believe**, **hear** *(mit den Ohren wahrnehmen)*, **know**, **like**, **mean**, **notice**, **see** *(mit den Augen wahrnehmen)*, **seem**, **want**, **wish**.

→ Merken Sie sich, dass die beiden Verben **see** und **hear** mit unterschiedlicher Bedeutung gebraucht werden. Wenn wir das Verb **see** im Sinne von „sich treffen“ und **hear** im Sinne von „etwas erfahren“ benutzen, dann kommt auch das Progressive in Frage.

Exercise 1 Fill in the progressive form where possible. In other cases you should put in the simple form. Use the given tenses.

1 We ____________________ Hamlet at the moment. *present: read*

2 After the exam I _____________ that I had left out one of the questions. *past: notice*

3 Mrs Gregg ______________________________ at the same address all her life. *present perfect: live*

4 This time yesterday I ______________________ an English test. *past: do*

5 I ________________ this film several times before.

↝ *present perfect: see*

6 Is that Richard Gray? I ________________________ a lot about him lately. ↝ *present perfect: hear*

7 The students _______________________ for their tutor for nearly an hour now. ↝ *present perfect: wait*

8 John ______________ Sheila almost every evening at present.

↝ *present: see*

2 Simple Present und Present Progressive im Vergleich

① People ~~are speaking~~ over 300 languages in India.
② Fred ~~is catching~~ a train to London every morning.
③ Sally and Miles can't come now. They ~~do~~ their homework.

❶ People **speak** over 300 languages in India.
❷ Fred **catches** a train to London every morning.
❸ Sally and Miles can't come now. They **are doing** their homework.

→ Ein häufiger Fehler ist, das Present Progressive bei **bestehenden Situationen oder Zuständen** zu gebrauchen. In solchen Fällen kommt nur das **Simple Present** in Frage ❶.

Sprechen wir von **Ausnahmefällen**, verwenden wir jedoch das **Present Progressive**:
I normally teach English but this year I **am teaching** French as well.

→ Bei sich **ständig wiederholenden Vorgängen** benutzen wir ebenfalls das **Simple Present** ❷.

→ Wir benutzen das **Present Progressive**, um zu verdeutlichen, dass die Handlung zur Zeit des Sprechens **im Gange** *(in progress)* ist. Im Deutschen benutzt man für diesen Zweck Ausdrücke wie „gerade", „im Augenblick" usw. ❸.

→ **Beachten** Sie: Das **Present Progressive** wird oft mit **always** verwendet, um sich über eine sich immer wiederholende Belästigung zu beklagen:
Our neighbours are awful. They **are always having** noisy parties.

Exercise 2 Use the simple present or the present progressive.

1 Now some Conservatives ____________________ that the UK should leave the EU. ⇝ *argue*

2 The new party ____________________ to win a lot of seats during the present elections. ⇝ *hope*

3 Recent surveys _____________ that British voters ____________ little interest in Northern Ireland. A lot of people ____________ to think the 'Troubles' ________ here to stay.

⇝ *show; have; seem; be*

4 Unfortunately politicians always _____________ the impression that they ___________ more power than _________ really the case.

⇝ *give; have; be*

5 It __________ here that the government ____________________ further tax cuts. ⇝ *say; plan*

6 Please be quiet. I ____________________ to listen to the news and you __________ making a noise. ⇝ *try; keep*

7 We ____________________ plenty of time. Look the traffic lights ____________________ red. ⇝ *have got; turn*

8 Jane Handy ____________________ all her own house repairs. Now she ____________________ in a new heating system. She ____________________ anybody, that is why she always ____________________ everything herself.

⇝ *do; put; not trust; do*

3 Das Simple Past und Past Progressive im Vergleich

① When Dad came home, we ~~already had~~ lunch.
② Fred didn't rob the bank. He ~~played~~ cards with me at the time.
③ The weather was beautiful last week. People ~~sunbathed~~ in the park.

❶ When Dad came home, we **were already having** lunch.
❷ Fred didn't rob the bank. He **was playing** cards with me at the time.
❸ The weather was beautiful last week. People **were sunbathing** in the park.

→ Wie wir gesehen haben, wird das Present Progressive überstrapaziert. Beim **Past Progressive** ist das gerade anders. Häufig wird das Simple Past anstelle des Progressive gebraucht.

→ Wir benutzen das **Past Progressive** in den folgenden beiden Fällen:
Um zu verdeutlichen, dass eine **Handlung schon im Gange** *(in progress)* war, als **ein neues Ereignis** eintrat ❶.
Um auszudrücken, dass eine Handlung zu einem bestimmten Zeitpunkt ❷ oder während eines bestimmten Zeitraumes ❸ **im Gange** war.

Vor allem in dem ersten Fall kann der falsche Gebrauch des Simple Past zu sinnentstellenden Fehlern führen.
Vergleichen Sie:
When the Prime Minister came in everybody **stood up**.
Als der Premierminister eintrat, standen alle auf.
When the Prime Minister came in everybody **was standing up**.
Als der Premierminister eintrat, standen schon alle.

Exercise 3 Use the simple past or the past progressive. Be careful about irregular forms and modal auxiliary verbs.

1 We ____________________ the test when the fire alarm ______________ and we all ____________________ the building. It __________ only a practice, but when we ________________ to the examination room we _____________ quite a surprise. One student ____________________ the teacher's bag. It ____________ he ____________________ to find the answers to the questions.

do; sound; must leave; be; return; have; search; seem; try

2 Jock ______________ into a lot of trouble today. When Mr Snow ________________ into his office, he ______________________

the firm's phone to call his sister in New Zealand. Jock __________ really silly. He __________________ with his back to the door so he ______________________ Mr Snow come in. When Jock finally __________ the phone down and __________________ round, Mr Snow ____________________ behind him.

get; come; use; be; sit; not see; put; turn; stand

3 I ________________________ past the school when two children __________ in front of my car. I ________________ them because they ______________ out from behind a big van. Luckily, I __________________ very slowly so I ____________________ in time and nothing __________________ .

drive; run; not see; come; drive; can stop; happen

Exercise 4 Translate the sentences into English.

1 *Wollen Sie meinen Regenschirm ausleihen? Es regnet gerade.*

____

____ .

2 *Ich habe meinen Finger verletzt, als ich das Gemüse vorbereitete.*

____

____ .

3 *Wie peinlich. Als wir ankamen, waren die Snows dabei, ins Bett zu gehen.*

____

____ .

4 *Leider muss ich jetzt weg. Jemand wartet auf mich am Flughafen.*

____

____ .

5 *Olaf liest viele englische Bücher. Im Moment liest er einen Bestseller von John le Carré.*

____

____

____ .

A 11 Grundfehler mit dem will- und going to-Futur

① Jill Mason ~~will fly~~ to New York.
② Watch out! That child ~~will run~~ across the road!
③ Our train ~~will leave~~ at 3 pm tomorrow.

✓ ❶ Jill Mason **is going to fly** to New York.
✓ ❷ Watch out! That child **is going to run** across the road!
✓ ❸ Our train **leaves** at 3 pm tomorrow.

→ Beim Futur ist der häufigste Fehler der Gebrauch von *will* statt **going to**. Beachten Sie deshalb, dass das **going to**-Futur für **feste Pläne**, die das Subjekt selbst gemacht hat, ❶ und für **Ereignisse,** die offensichtlich in allernächster Zeit eintreten werden ❷, zwingend ist.

Beachten Sie: Enthält der Satz ein **Adverb der Zeit** wie **this afternoon**, **tomorrow**, **next week** usw. bevorzugt man bei ❶ das **Present Progressive.**
Jill Mason **is flying** to New York **next week**.

→ Eine weitere Fehlerquelle ist die Tendenz, das *will*-Futur für Vorgänge, die in Fahrplänen, Programmen, Stundenplänen usw. festgelegt sind, zu gebrauchen. In solchen Fällen benutzen wir im Englischen – wie im Deutschen – das **Simple Present** ❸.

Exercise 1 Look at the parts in italics of the situations. Would the speakers use the **will**-future or the **going to**-future?

1 Ein Polizist steht am Straßenrand. Er sieht Sally genau in die Augen. Sie ist sicher, dass *er sie anhalten wird*.

____

2 Eine Nachbarin sagt, dass ihre Tochter am kommenden Mittwoch *zehn Jahre alt wird*.

____

3 Tom will Sarah sagen, dass er sie heute Abend *bei einem gemeinsamen Freund sehen wird*.

____

4 Tony will seiner Frau sagen, dass er sich entschieden hat, *in nächster Zeit eine neue Stelle zu suchen*.

____

5 Ein Vertreter ruft bei einer Firma an, um zu sagen, dass er wegen einer Autopanne *nicht vor 15 Uhr ankommt*.

____

Exercise 2 Use the elements to make sentences with the present progressive with future meaning or **going to**. Use the progressive only when there is an adverb of future time. You must add the missing articles, prepositions etc as necessary.

I / have / baby
I'm going to have a baby.

1 Tom and Mary / get / divorce

____.

2 we / not take / holiday / next year

____.

3 firm / open / office / Erfurt / next month

____.

4 we / have / barbecue / on Saturday

____.

5 government / bring in / new law / control / use / drugs

____

____.

6 education authorities / introduce / new exams / beginning / next school year

____

____.

Exercise 3 Translate the sentences into English.

1 *Die Wettervorhersage sagt, dass es morgen sonnig wird.*

____

____.

2 *Mein Bruder fliegt am 10. August nach Florida.*

____.

3 *Morgen kann ich nicht kommen. Mein Zug fährt um 11 Uhr 30.*

____.

4 *Ich vermute, dass wir einen guten Preis für unsere Wohnung bekommen.*

____.

5 *Wird Tom einen neuen Wagen kaufen?*

____.

A 12 Typische Gundfehler mit Strukturwörtern

1 *There* + Form von *be*

① ~~A lot of statistics are~~ in the text.
② Listen! ~~Somebody is~~ in the garden.
③ Most scientists think ~~it gives no~~ life on Mars.

✓ ❶ **There are** a lot of statistics in the text.
✓ ❷ Listen! **There is** somebody in the garden.
✓ ❸ Most scientists think **there is** no life on Mars.

→ Bei relativ vielen Ausdrucksfehlern handelt es sich um den falschen Gebrauch von **there + einer Form von be**. Mit dieser Struktur, die in allen Zeiten verwendet werden kann, drücken wir aus, dass das **nachfolgende Subjekt vorhanden** ❶, ❷ oder **existent** ❸ ist.

→ Im Deutschen wird diese Idee unterschiedlich ausgedrückt, daher kommt es häufig zu Fehlern:
There is nobody at home, I'm afraid.
Leider ist keiner zu Hause.
There are several convincing arguments for legalizing drugs.
Es gibt mehrere überzeugende Argumente für die Legalisierung von Drogen.
Were there many people at the lecture?
Waren viele Menschen bei dem Vortrag?
I'm sure **there will be** a question about the environment.
Ich bin sicher, dass es eine Frage zum Thema Umwelt geben wird.

Exercise 1 Finish translating the sentences into English. Be careful. Some of them do not require **there** + **be**.

1 *Es ist irgendetwas falsch mit diesem Satz.*

________________________________ with this sentence.

2 *Gestern gab es eine große Demonstration in Bonn.*

________________________________ in Bonn yesterday.

3 *Es waren viele Menschen in der Stadt heute.*

________________________________ in town today.

4 *Es war sehr nett von Ihnen, mich nach Hause zu fahren.*

________________________________ to drive me home.

5 *Entschuldigen Sie, bitte. Gibt es eine Tankstelle in der Nähe?*

Excuse me, please. ________________________ near here?

6 *Meinst Du, dass es auch Fragen zu „Hamlet“ geben wird?*

Do you think ________________________________ on “Hamlet”?

7 *Es ist schwierig, Peters Meinung zu Immigranten zu teilen.*

______________________________ Peter’s opinion on immigrants.

8 *Es sind viele Steaks übrig geblieben. Es hat keinen Zweck, mehr Fleisch zu kaufen.*

___________________________ left over. ______________

_________ in buying more meat.

2 *What, which oder who?*

① ~~Which films~~ have you seen this year?
② ~~Which people~~ voted for the Greens?
③ ~~What do~~ you like most, this T-shirt or that one?

✓ ❶ **What films** have you seen this year?
✓ ❷ **Who** voted for the Greens?
✓ ❸ **Which T-shirt** do you like most, this one or that one?

→ Einige leicht vermeidbare Fehler sind auf den unterschiedlichen Gebrauch von **what**, **which** und **who** in Fragesätzen zurückzuführen. Mit **what** fragen wir nach **Sachen** ❶, mit **who** nach **Personen** ❷ aus einer **unbeschränkten Zahl**.
Mit **which** fragen wir nach **Sachen** ❸ und **Personen** aus einer **beschränkten Auswahl**.

→ Merken Sie sich, dass **which** sehr häufig vor einer **of**-Fügung steht. Diese Struktur entspricht dem Deutschen „*Wer von euch / Ihnen …?*“

Exercise 2 Fill in **what, which** or **who.**

1 ___________ sports are most popular in the UK?

2 ___________ did you talk to most at Greg’s party?

3 ___________ were you speaking to on the phone just now?

4 ___________ countries are against the abolition of passports?

5 ___________ candidate do you think is most suitable for this job?

6 ___________ of the arguments did the group find most convincing?

3 *Too* oder *either*?

① I don't like westerns and I ~~don't like also~~ sci-fi films.
② Fred never reads a book and Harry ~~doesn't too~~.

✓ ❶ I don't like westerns and I **don't like** sci-fi films, **either**.
✓ ❷ Fred never reads a book and Harry **doesn't**, **either**.

→ Bei Fehlern im Zusammenhang mit **too** / **either** handelt es sich meist um **either**.

Der Gebrauch von **too** in **bejahten Aussagen** und **Fragen** ist unproblematisch:
We **are reading** Macbeth at the moment, **too**.
Do you hope to go to university, **too?**

Wir benutzen **either** in **verneinten Aussagen** ❶, ❷.

→ Beachten Sie, dass beide Wörter gewöhnlich **am Satzende** stehen und durch ein **Komma** vom übrigen Satz getrennt werden.

Exercise 3 Put in **too** or **either**. Don't forget the comma.

1 If their son can't have a car, they shouldn't buy their daughter one either.

2 Bob has got a bad memory. At the time he liked the idea too.

3 Does the Czech Republic want to join the EU too?

4 Nobody in Europe can accept chaining prisoners together either.

5 There had been no time to tidy up, and no reason to do so either.

6 He had not yet spoken to her or looked at her either.

4 Die Stützwörter *one / ones*

① Do you want the red T-shirt, or the ~~green~~?
② I enjoy thrillers but I don't like unnecessarily violent ~~thrillers~~.
③ Did you buy some apples? Yes. Six ~~ones~~.

✓ ❶ Do you want the red T-shirt, or the green **one**?
✓ ❷ I enjoy thrillers but I don't like unnecessarily violent **ones**.
✓ ❸ Did you buy some apples? Yes. **Six**.

→ Da es im Deutschen möglich ist, ein Adjektiv allein zu benutzen, gibt es keine Entsprechung für die Stützwörter **one** (Singular) und **ones** (Plural). Daher sind die klassischen Fehler entweder das Stützwort einfach auszulassen ❶ oder das Substantiv unnötig zu wiederholen ❷.

→ Beachten Sie aber:
Nach **Kardinalzahlen** verwenden wir grundsätzlich **kein Stützwort** ❸.

→ Nach **Superlativen** wie **the best**, **the most popular** usw., nach **Ordinalzahlen** und nach **which** können wir das Stützwort weglassen.

Exercise 4 Complete the sentence with **one** / **ones** where necessary or put a cross (**x**) in the space where no prop word is needed. Underline the relevant noun in each case.

1 I tried to get you a German newspaper but the shop didn't have ________ .

2 James Wyatt's new book isn't nearly as good as his last ________ .

3 You can't miss Ingrid's house. It's the ________ with a telephone box in the garden.

4 We've got dozens of batteries. Which ________ do you need?

5 I enjoyed both films but I thought the second ________ was a little too long.

6 Why on earth did you buy Dutch tomatoes? I asked you to get French ________ .

7 The shop had jeans from £20 to £150. Of course, Sarah had to buy the most expensive ________ .

8 We didn't go to the Chinese restaurant. We went to the ________ in Frith Street.

5 *Each* oder *every?*

① Jo goes to the health club ~~each~~ night.
② ~~Every~~ partner in a marriage should be polite and tolerant.
③ The workers got ~~every~~ a bonus of £1000.

✓ ❶ Jo goes to the health club **every** night.
✓ ❷ **Each partner** in a marriage should be polite and tolerant.
✓ ❸ The workers got a bonus of £1000 **each.**

→ Die Wörter **each** und **every** entsprechen dem deutschen jede / -r / -s. Oft sind sie – besonders in der modernen Umgangssprache – austauschbar. Beachten Sie aber folgende Fälle, die oft zu Fehlern führen:

→ Wenn von der Intention her der Sprecher sich eindeutig in einem ganz **allgemeinen, allumfassenden Sinn** äußert, dann muß **every** verwendet werden ❶:
Nobody escaped. The police caught **everyone** in the building.

→ Von der Logik her ist **each** die einzige Möglichkeit bei einer **Auswahl von zweien** ❷:
The Greens have got **two** dogs and **each** won a prize at the dog show.

→ Wir können nur **each** allein ❸ oder vor einer **of**-Fügung benutzen:
There were over 500 visitors and **each** received a free catalogue.
Each of the speakers argued for a law to protect minorities.

Exercise 5 Complete the sentences with **each** or **every**. Where both are possible, use both.

1 ________ time I see Ben he seems to be in a bad temper.
2 ________ member of the UN has a seat in the general assembly.
3 ________ motor cycle is checked carefully and ________ gets an OK-sticker.
4 ________ of the texts was about some aspect of the USA.
5 Nobody was allowed to go until ________ had shown their passport.
6 ________ single student in my group did well in the exam.

6 Verben mit einer *to*-Fügung (indirektem Objekt)

① Mrs Adams ~~dictated the class the homework~~.
② The boy ~~described me the way.~~
③ Let me ~~explain it you.~~

✓ ❶ Mrs Adams **dictated the homework to the class**.
✓ ❷ The boy **described the way to me**.
✓ ❸ Let me **explain it to you**.

→ Ein relativ häufiger Fehler ist der Versuch, eine kleine Gruppe von Verben – meist Verben der Mitteilung – mit einem unmittelbar angeschlossenem indirekten Objekt zu gebrauchen.

→ Verben wie **dictate** ❶, **describe** ❷ und **explain** ❸ können keine zwei Objekte haben. Die Person, der irgendetwas mitgeteilt wird, kann nur mit der Präposition **to** direkt hinter dem Objekt angeschlossen werden:

Subjekt	Verb	Objekt	to-Fügung
Mrs Adams	dictated	the homework	**to** the class.
The boy	described	the way	**to** me.
Let me	explain	it	**to** you.

Andere Verben dieser Gruppe sind:

announce The company **announced** its plans **to the press**. *(ankündigen)*
deliver We can't **deliver** the books **to the shop** before Friday. *(liefern)*
distribute Can you **distribute** this letter **to all the pupils**, please? *(verteilen)*
introduce May I **introduce** Janet Scott **to you**? *(vorstellen)*
mention Joan didn't **mention** her illness **to her husband**. *(erwähnen)*
present The writer **presented** his new book **to the audience**. *(präsentieren)*
say Don't **say** rude things like that **to people**. *(sagen)*
suggest Sarah **suggested** going to the cinema **to the children**. *(vorschlagen)*

→ Beachten Sie aber: Bei Verben mit einem indirekten Objekt und einem direkten Objekt wie **bring**, **give**, **lend**, **send**, **take** usw. steht das indirekte Objekt an erster Stelle **ohne to**:

Subjekt	Verb	indirektes Objekt	direktes Objekt
Tony	gave	Sally	a kiss.
The bank	lent	the Harpers	a lot of money.

→ Nach **tell** steht immer ein **indirektes Objekt**:
The frontier guard **told the tourists** to give him their passports.

Exercise 6 Put the indirect objects into the sentences. Use **to** as necessary.

1 Did you lend ________ your car last weekend?
→ *Ben*

2 How can they understand the problem if you don't explain it ________ ? → *them*

3 The minister told ________ the government's plan.
→ *the MPs*

4 Won't you introduce your new boyfriend ________ , Sally? → *us*

5 Mr Coe announced ________ that he was retiring. → *the meeting*

6 Oh dear. The Snows are going to show ________ their photos.
→ *the guests*

7 Ben phoned ________ about the car repairs. → *the mechanic*

8 Chris didn't mention the new project ________
→ *the authors*

9 Carr & Co distribute their products ________ all over the world. → *customers*

10 Jack suggested ________ that he took a flat of his own. → *his parents*

11 Don't tell ________ Why don't you say all this ________ ? → *me, your wife*

12 Don't forget to write ________ today, will you?
→ *Granny*

13 Could you ask ________ for the menu, please?
→ *the waiter*

B

Vierzehn weitere Gruppen von oft gemachten Fehlern

B 1 Fehler mit Adjektiven und Adverbien

1 Die Adverbform von *-ly*-Adjektiven

① Shop assistants should always ~~speak~~ to customers ~~friendly.~~
② The girls are OK but the boys often ~~behave silly.~~

✓ ❶ Shop assistants should always **speak to customers in a friendly way**.
✓ **or:** Shop assistants should always **be friendly to customers**.
✓ ❷ The girls are OK but the boys often **behave in a silly way**.
✓ **or:** The girls are OK but the boys **are often silly**.

→ Eine weitere Fehlerquelle bei Adverbien ist auf die Adverbform von Adjektiven, die auf -ly enden, zurückzuführen. Einige Englischlernende meinen, dass – weil eben das Adjektiv schon auf -ly endet –, keine weitere Umformung notwendig ist ❶, ❷.

→ Bei solchen Adjektiven gibt es **zwei Möglichkeiten**: Wir können das Muster **in a** + -**ly**-**Adjektiv** + **way** mit dem Verb benutzen (in den ersten Sätzen von ❶, ❷) oder wir können das ursprüngliche Verb durch **be** ersetzen und dann mit dem Adjektiv benutzen – jeweils der zweite Satz von ❶, ❷.

→ Andere wichtige -ly-Adjektive, die nicht ohne weiteres als Adverbien benutzt werden können, sind:
cowardly *(feige)*, **deadly**, **lonely**, **lovely** *(liebenswert)*, **ugly** *(häßlich)*

Exercise 1 Put the English equivalent of the German adverbs into the sentences. Use the expression **in a** ... **way** where necessary.

☼ The mother sang to her child **in a lovely way**. ⇝ *liebenswert*

Please get on with your work **quietly**. ⇝ *ruhig*

1 The hijackers threatened the passengers ______________________ .
⇝ *hässlich*

2 Please don't talk ________________ in the cathedral. ⇝ *laut*

3 I think that some fashion models walk ______________________ .
⇝ *blöd*

4 Everybody knows that bullies behave ______________________ .
⇝ *feige*

5 You should drive ____________ in residential areas. ⇝ *langsam*

6 Sally is very conscientious. She does everything _______________ .
⇝ *gründlich*

2 Adverbien mit zwei Formen von unterschiedlicher Bedeutung

① John is training ~~hardly~~ for the match.
② They repair new cars ~~freely~~ for the first year.

✓ ❶ John is training **hard** for the competition.
*Im Moment trainiert John **hart** für den Wettbewerb.*
✓ **or:** You can **hardly** expect Wendy to accept Tom's behaviour.
*Man kann **kaum** erwarten, dass Wendy Toms Benehmen akzeptiert.*
✓ ❷ They repair new cars **free** for the first year.
*Sie reparieren neue Wagen **kostenlos** im ersten Jahr.*
✓ **or:** Apply the cleaner **freely** to the dirty places.
*Tragen Sie das Reinigungsmittel **großzügig** auf die verschmutzten Stellen auf.*

→ Merken Sie sich, dass einige Adverbien **zwei Formen** haben, eine wie **das Adjektiv** und eine auf -**ly**.
Die beiden Formen haben jedoch **unterschiedliche Bedeutungen**, die Sie nicht verwechseln sollten.
Die wichtigsten Adverbien dieser Art sind:

close	*nah*	**closely**	*genau, sorgfältig*
direct	*direkt*	**directly**	*sofort*
free	*kostenlos*	**freely**	*freizügig*
hard	*hart*	**hardly**	*kaum*
high	*hoch*	**highly**	*sehr viel, höchst-*
just	*gerade, soeben*	**justly**	*gerecht, rechtmäßig*
late	*spät*	**lately**	*neulich*
near	*nah*	**nearly**	*fast*
pretty	*ziemlich*	**prettily**	*hübsch*
wide	*weit*	**widely**	*an vielen Orten, weit verbreitet*

Exercise 2 Put the English equivalent of the German into the sentences.

1 Two ____________________ were ________________________ in the explosion. *ältere Fußgänger; ziemlich ernsthaft verletzt*

2 It is ______________________ that ______________ feel themselves ____________________________ .
kaum überraschend; die Armen; ungerecht behandelt

3 You can't cross the Polish-German border ________________ . The border guards look _____________________ at everybody's papers. *freizügig; sehr genau*

4 I am ______________ that we have ______________ finished ____________________ . *froh; fast; dieses langweilige Stück*

5 Contact staff are ______________ expected to treat customers ______________________ . natürlich; freundlich

6 It is ________________________________ that __________ __________ have caused ______________________ in schools.
eine weitverbreitete Meinung; große Klassen; die wachsende Krise

7 It is ______________________ that we have ______________ seen how ______________ NATO ______________ is.
schwer zu verleugnen; neulich; machtlos; eigentlich

Exercise 3 This is an extract from a company image-brochure. Complete the text with adjectives and adverbs from the list

Stora Kabel GmbH is a paper maker in Hagen. The company belongs to the Stora Billerud Group, one of Europe's ______________ manufacturers of ______________________ paper.

Located at the mouth of the Lenne, Stora Kabel covers an area of ______________ 500,000 square metres. Today, the 1,100 jobs offered by the company play an ________________ part in the life of the region. Our employees enjoy living in Hagen – a lively town ___________ to the beautiful Sauerland – because along with the _____________ quality of life Stora Kabel offers attractive and __________ employment. Our expectations are _________ but the work is interesting and ______________ and salaries are ________________________ . Since 1959 ________________ two billion marks have been invested in the Kabel plant to meet the demands of a __________________ market. As a result of this _________ investment, ___________ production has increased ________ from 185 tonnes per day in 1960 to 1,500 tonnes today.

close, daily, fast-developing, high, high, high-quality, huge, important, most advanced, nearly, nearly, performance-related, secure, steadily, varied

B 2 Fehler mit Present, Past und Present Perfect

1 Simple Present und Present Perfect im Vergleich

① Sarah ~~lives~~ here ~~since~~ two years.
② I ~~visit~~ my brother in America every summer since 1992.

✓ ❶ Sarah **has lived** here **for** two years.
✓ ❷ I **have visited** my brother in America every summer since 1992.

→ Wegen der Abweichung vom Deutschen ist der weitaus häufigste Fehler die Anwendung des **Simple Present** statt des **Present Perfect** mit andauernden Zuständen ❶ bzw. Handlungen ❷.
Ein weiterer Fehler ist die Verwendung von **since** statt **for** bei Zeiträumen ❶.

→ Wenn wir ausdrücken wollen, dass irgendetwas in der Vergangenheit anfing und bis in die Gegenwart andauert, benutzen wir im Englischen das **Present Perfect**.
Um zu verdeutlichen, dass es sich um eine **fortlaufende Situation** handelt, verwenden wir dabei **immer eine Zeitangabe** wie **before now** / **today** / …, **for three days** / **two years** / **several months** / … (**Zeitdauer**), **since July** / **last week** / **1993** / … (**Zeitpunkt**), **so far**, **so far today** / **this year** / …, **up till now**, **up to the present** usw.

Exercise 1 Complete the table with adverbs of time from the list.

all my life, always, before now, day after day, every Easter, for several weeks, from time to time, occasionally, regularly, since I was a child, seldom, so far this morning, the whole afternoon, up till this moment, up to today, usually

simple present	present perfect

Exercise 2 Underline the adverb of time where possible and then fill in the simple present or the present perfect of the verbs.

1 Sarah ______________ in London since her marriage. ↝ *live*

2 Ben seldom __________ meat. He ______________ on a special diet for months. ↝ *eat; be*

3 I always ______________ for lessons but my teacher never __________ me any questions. ↝ *prepare; ask*

4 The Royal Shakespeare Company ____________________ Shakespeare. It ____________________ several new plays during the last few seasons. ↝ *not only do; perform*

5 When you ________________ the test, you ________________ me your paper and leave the room. ↝ *finish; can give*

6 I ________________ to Joe about his work several times and he ______________ to be trying harder now. ↝ *speak; seem*

7 You ______________ the doctor in a moment, Mrs Simms. She ________________________ . ↝ *can see; just + arrive*

8 I ________________ Jane ever since she was a baby but I ____________________ her for years. ↝ *know; not see*

2 Simple Past und Present Perfect im Vergleich

① Sarah can't play hockey today. She ~~(recently) hurt~~ her leg.
② I'm sorry. Dr Jones isn't here. She ~~(just) went~~ home.
③ ~~Did~~ you ~~see~~ this film?

✓ ❶ Sarah can't play hockey today. She **has** (recently) **hurt** her leg.
✓ ❷ I'm sorry. Dr Jones isn't here. She **has** (just) **gone** home.
✓ ❸ **Have** you **seen** this film?

→ Wollen wir zum Ausdruck bringen, dass eine wichtige Verbindung zwischen einer **vergangenen Handlung** bzw. **Situation** und der **Gegenwart** besteht, dann benutzen wir im Englischen das **Present Perfect** ❶, ❷.

→ Um zu verdeutlichen, dass wir uns eher für das **gegenwärtige Ergebnis** interessieren, können wir eine Zeitangabe wie **already**, **before**, **just**, (**not**) **yet**, **still** (**not**) benutzen.
Häufig kommen wir jedoch ohne Zeitangabe ❸ aus.

Exercise 3 Use the simple past or the present perfect.

1 Sarah ____________ a good night's sleep since she ____________ birth to her baby. *not have; give*

2 Shakespeare ____________ on several plays at the same time and ____________ an actor-manager as well. He even ____________ and ____________ the Globe Theatre in London. *work; be; design; build*

3 In the debate last week some MPs ____________ to know why the government ____________ nothing about illegal immigration. In reply, a minister ____________ that the government ____________ more controls at ports and immigration officials ____________ told to be stricter.
want; do; say; introduce; be

4 "How long ____________ the Greens?"
"About two years. We ____________ on holiday in Greece and we ____________ quite a lot of them since then."
you / know; meet; see

5 The research I ____________ last week ____________ that anti-discrimination laws ____________ little effect. The situation of most women ____________ and those few women who ____________ to get better jobs only ____________ them because they had an unfair advantage over men.
read; claim; have; not improve; manage; get

6 In 1995 the Queen ____________ South Africa for the first time since the country ____________ the Commonwealth.
That ____________ in 1962.
The last time the Queen ____________ there she ____________ a teenager.
visit; leave; happen; be; be

3 Present Perfect und Present Perfect Progressive im Vergleich

① The Snows ~~are cleaning / clean~~ their car the whole afternoon.
② Poor Mrs Flint ~~has waited~~ for the bus for over an hour.
③ Tom and Mary ~~have been knowing~~ each other since they were at college.

✓ ❶ The Snows **have been cleaning** their car **the whole afternoon.**
✓ ❷ Poor Mrs Flint **has been waiting** for the bus **for over an hour.**
✓ ❸ Tom and Mary **have known** each other since they were at college.

→ Fehler bei der Anwendung des **Present Perfect Progressive** beruhen auf drei Ursachen:
Die Tendenz eine Zeitform des Präsens statt des **Present Perfect Progressive** zu benutzen ❶.
Der Gebrauch der einfachen Form des Present Perfect statt des **Present Perfect Progressive** bei lang andauernden Handlungen ❷.
Die Anwendung des Progressive mit Verben, die **nie** in der Progressive Form benutzt werden können ❸ (siehe auch Seite 51).

→ Möchten wir ausdrücken, dass eine Tätigkeit in der **Vergangenheit anfing und noch andauert**, dann benutzen wir das **Present Perfect Progressive**.

→ Merken Sie sich, dass wir das **Present Perfect Progressive** nur bei Tätigkeiten, die über einen längeren Zeitraum ausgeübt werden können wie **argue**, **learn**, **lie**, **live**, **play**, **quarrel**, **rain**, **snow**, **sit**, **sleep**, **stand**, **wait**, **work**, benutzen.
Oft findet man bei dieser Zeitform Adverbien wie **all day** / **month** / **week** / …, **for ages** / **a** (**very**) **long time**, (**ever**) **since I have known him**, **the whole time**.

Exercise 4 Translate the sentences into English. Use the present perfect progressive.

1 *Die Greggs streiten sich schon wieder den ganzen Vormittag.*

____

____ .

2 *Frau Coe wohnt hier, seit sie ein kleines Mädchen war.*

____

____ .

3 *Es regnet jetzt schon seit Wochen.*

____ .

4 *Du schläft seit einer Ewigkeit.*

____ .

5 *Dieser Roman ist zu lang. Wir lesen ihn jetzt schon seit Anfang März.*

____

____ .

6 *Der Präsident regiert seit über einem Jahr durch Dekret (by decree).*

____

____ .

Exercise 5 Fill in the present perfect or the present perfect progressive.

1 I ____________________ my brother since he moved to the USA. ↝ *not see*

2 Drivers who ________________________ their test are particularly likely to have accidents. ↝ *just + pass*

3 The employers and the unions ________________________ all night but they ________________________ an agreement.
↝ *negotiate; still + not reach*

4 Poor Julie ____________________ her driving test again. Now she ____________________ to give up and go by bus.
↝ *fail; decide*

5 The police ____________________ the protestant marches this year but the protestants ____________________ to obey. They say that they ____________________ through the town every 12 July for over two hundred years. ↝ *forbid; refuse; march*

6 I ________________________ Hugh Grant's new film yet. Would you like to come and see it with me?
↝ *not see*

7 Ted came for a short stay six months ago and he ________________________ with us ever since.
↝ *live*

B 3 Was es beim Futur noch zu beachten gibt

1 Weitere Anwendungen von *will*

① Listen to me. You ~~are~~ home at 10 and that's that, OK?
② Don't come round this afternoon. I think Greg ~~is~~ out then.
③ The car ~~doesn't start~~. We ~~must~~ walk.

✓ ❶ Listen to me. You **will be** home at 10 and that's that, OK?
✓ ❷ Don't come round this afternoon. I think Greg **will be** out then.
✓ ❸ The car **won't start**. We**'ll have to walk**.

→ Oft wird analog zum Deutschen das Simple Present verwendet, wenn im Englischen das **will-Futur** stehen **muss**. Diese Art Fehler kommt vor allem in den folgenden Fällen vor:

Bei Anordnungen oder Befehlen, die als **Vorhersagen** ausgedrückt werden ❶:
Benny, you **will tidy up** your room before you do anything else.
Benny, du räumst dein Zimmer auf, bevor du irgend etwas anderes tust.

Bei Vermutungen über **zukünftige Ereignisse** ❷:
I suppose we **will have to invite** the Snows, too.
Ich nehme an, dass wir auch die Snows einladen müssen.

Bei der Feststellung eines **Zustandes und dessen Auswirkung** ❸:
Mrs Coe **will be afraid** to open the door. I **will phone** her first.
Mrs Coe wird Angst haben, die Tür zu öffnen. Ich rufe vorher an.

→ Merken Sie sich, dass bei **Nebensätzen**, die sich auf eine **zukünftige Handlung beziehen**, wir im Nebensatz – nicht jedoch im Hauptsatz – das **Simple Present** verwenden:
I'll ring when the car **is** ready.
Ich rufe an, wenn das Auto fertig ist.
We **will write** again as soon as we **know** more.
Wir schreiben wieder, sobald wir mehr wissen.

Exercise 1 Use the letters to say what use of the **will**-future the sentences exemplify.
a Befehl, **b** Erwartung, **c** Feststellung, **d** Hoffnung, **e** plötzliche Entscheidung, **f** Vorhersage

1 I'm sure that all MPs will support the peace process. ____

2 You've missed the bus? Don't worry. I'll drive you home. ____

3 All visitors will register at the information desk before going further.

____

4 Critics of privatization say it will lead to falling standards of care.

____

5 We can't go cycling tomorrow. The forecast said it will be over 35°C.

____

6 There will be riots unless something is done for the unemployed.

____

Exercise 2 Finish translating the sentences into English.

1 *Jener Koffer ist viel zu schwer. Ich helfe dir.*

That case is much too heavy. ______________________ .

2 *Der Autor meint, dass die Regierung das Gesetz ändert.*

The author thinks that the government ______________________ .

3 *Meinen Sie, dass Privatisierung zu Preiserhöhungen führen wird?*

Do you think that ______________________________________

______________________________ ?

2 Das Future Progressive und Future Perfect

① I needn't write to Sean. I ~~see~~ him at the meeting on Friday.
② John's very ill. He ~~won't come~~ to work for several months.
③ This time tomorrow we ~~fly / will fly~~ to Florida.

✓ ❶ I needn't write to Sean. I **will be seeing** him at the meeting on Friday.
✓ ❷ John's very ill. He **won't be coming** to work for several months.
✓ ❸ This time tomorrow we **will be flying** to Florida.

→ Der Standardfehler bei der Anwendung des **Future Progressive** ist, auf diese Zeitform – meist zu Gunsten des Simple Present oder des einfachen Futurs – völlig zu verzichten.

Beachten Sie, dass wir das **Future Progressive** wie folgt einsetzen: Wenn ein zukünftiges Ereignis **mit Bestimmtheit** eintreten wird ❶, ❷. Hier kann man auch das Present Progressive mit einem verstärkenden Adverb wie **certainly**, **definitely**, **without a doubt** usw. anwenden. Jane **will be visiting** us at Easter. / Jane **is definitely visiting** us at Easter.

Wenn wir sagen wollen, dass eine Handlung zu einem bestimmten zukünftigen Zeitpunkt im Gange sein wird ❸.

→ Auch bei dem **Future Perfect (will have + 3. Form des Vollverbs)** ist der häufigste Fehler die falsche Anwendung des einfachen Futurs statt des Future Perfect.
Beachten Sie deshalb: Wollen wir sagen, dass eine Handlung zu einem bestimmten **zukünftigen Zeitpunkt bereits abgeschlossen** sein wird, benutzen wir das **Future Perfect**.

Aus diesem Grund kommt das **Future Perfect** oft mit **Adverbien** wie **a week** / **year** / **... from now**, **before Christmas** / **the coming school year** / ..., **by July** / **Easter** / ... (**nicht** *until*), **next Friday** / **autumn** / ... **this time tomorrow** / **next year** / ... usw. vor.

→ Hier sind drei weitere Beispiele für den Gebrauch des **Future Perfects**:
Next November the Prime Minister **will have been** in office for five years.
Nächsten November wird der Premierminister seit fünf Jahren im Amt sein.
Lord Nolan **will have completed** his report **before the summer**.
Lord Nolan wird seinen Bericht vor dem Sommer abgeschlossen haben.
Will you have saved enough money **by August**?
Wirst du bis August genügend Geld gespart haben?

Exercise 3 Make sentences with the elements. Add the missing articles and prepositions. Use the future progressive.

☀ minister / make / announcement / shortly
The minister will be making an announcement shortly.

1 next July / we / visit / our relatives / USA

Next July we ______________________________ .

2 they / still + repair / car / 3 o'clock

They ______________________________ .

3 I / see / Sean / beginning / August

I ______________________________ .

4 Brenda / collect / those statistics / months

Brenda ______________________________ .

5 you + attend / meeting / tomorrow / ?

______________________________ ?

6 Mr Carr / ask / your opinion / within / next few days

Mr Carr ______________________________ .

7 this time / tomorrow afternoon / we / drive Leeds

Tomorrow afternoon ______________________________

______________________________ .

Exercise 4 Now use the future perfect.

we / finish / novel / May
We will have finished the novel by May.

1 East Germany / not catch up / West Germany / another generation

East Germany ______________________________

______________________________ .

2 you + complete / job / 5 o'clock / ?

______________________________ ?

3 Sue / work / here / over 40 years / end / month

Sue ______________________________ .

4 Don't worry. you / definitely + receive / new passport / then

Don't worry. You ______________________________

______________________________ .

Exercise 5 Complete the dialogue. Use **will**-future (7), present progressive (3), simple present (2) and **going to**-future (1).

TOM: ____________ anything this weekend, Ann? *you / do*

ANN: It depends. Saturday is out. I ____________ to York in the morning and then in the afternoon I ____________ ____ somebody in hospital. *go; visit*

TOM: OK, what about Saturday evening? A super new film ____________ at the Odeon tomorrow. *start*

ANN: Oh, Tom. I ____________ so tired and I know I ________ ________ like going out. Anyhow, there ________ some good programmes on TV on Saturday. I'm sorry. I think I ______ ________ at home. *be; not feel; be; stay*

TOM: Oh, come on, Ann. I ____________ you what – I ______ ________ and get you at 8 and then we ____________ the gang at the club for a beer. *tell; come; meet*

ANN: OK, Tom. But I ____________ in a pub all night. *not stand*

TOM: Fine, we ____________ for an hour. *just + stay*

B 4 Fehler mit dem Passiv

1 Form

① Sarah ~~was stopping~~ for speeding.
② Two Europeans ~~have~~ just ~~arrested~~ for smuggling drugs.
③ Stamps ~~can bought~~ at the corner shop.

✓ ❶ Sarah **was stopped** for speeding.
✓ ❷ Two Europeans **have just been arrested** for smuggling drugs.
✓ ❸ Stamps **can be bought** at the corner shop.

→ Bei den weitaus meisten Fehlern mit dem Passiv geht es nicht um den Gebrauch, sondern um die **Form** ❶, ❷. Dies ist besonders der Fall bei Passivsätzen, die mit **modalen Hilfsverben** gebildet werden ❸.

→ Das Passiv wird mit einer Form von **be** und der **3. Form eines Vollverbs** gebildet:

Zeitform	Subjekt	Form von be	Vollverb	andere Teile
Simple Present	This car	is	**made**	in Japan.
	The computers	are	**manufactured**	in the USA.
Present Progressive	Our flat	is being	**decorated**	at the moment.
	The books	are being	**delivered**	today.
Simple Past	This church	was	**built**	in 1145.
	The houses	were	**renovated**	last year.
Past Progressive	The lift	was being	**repaired**	all day Monday.
	The passengers	were being	**checked in**	when we arrived.
Present Perfect	Our car	has been	**repaired**	twice this year.
	Some film stars	have been	**divorced**	several times.
Past Perfect	Jane said her car	had been	**broken into**	again.
Will-future	The minister says taxes	will be	**reduced**	soon.
Conditional I	They told us we	would be	**paid**	more money.
Conditional II	The child	could have been	**saved**	by quick action.

→ Passivkonstruktionen mit **Modalverben** werden mit dem **Modalverb** + **be** + **3. Form des Vollverbs** gebildet:

Zeit	Subjekt	Modalverb	be	Vollverb	andere Teile
Present	Tickets	must	be	**cancelled**	before getting on the train.
Past	The film	was not allowed to	be	**broadcast**	before 10 pm.
Will-future	Seats	will have to	be	**provided**	for all spectators in future.

→ Einige Fehler werden durch die falsche Stellung von Adverbien in Passivsätzen verursacht. Merken Sie sich deshalb, dass die Adverbstellung genau dieselbe wie bei Aktivsätzen ist (siehe Seite 48):

Subjekt	be	Adverb	Verb	andere Teile
The house	**was**	**completely**	**redecorated**	last year.
Mr Snow	**has been**	**urgently**	**advised**	to give up smoking.
I	**am**	**currently**	**being considered**	for a new job.
Passports	**must be**	**carefully**	**examined**	at the border.

Exercise 1 Fill in the correct form of the passive. Use the tense given. Be careful about the position of adverbs.

1 When the guests arrived, they ______________________________ to their rooms. *simple past: immediately + show*

2 It ______________________________ that women learn faster than men. *present perfect: recently + suggest*

3 After the meeting ______________________________ , the chairman gave his report. *past perfect: formally + open*

4 A vast amount of waste ________________ into the North Sea every day. *simple present: tip*

5 Can you stay in a hotel? Our bedrooms ______________________ ____________ at the moment. *present progressive: decorate*

6 Bosnia proves that countries ______________________ purely geographically. Unfortunately, ethnic questions ________________ ________________ .
simple present: can / not create; also + must / consider

7 This fact ______________________________ into account by the EU. *present perfect: really + not take*

8 The British Conservatives ______________________________ over Europe for years. *present perfect: seriously + divide*

9 However, new voluntary recommendations ________________ ____________ shortly. *will-future: publish*

2 Der *by-agent*

① The epic poem "Paradise Lost" was written ~~from~~ Milton.
② Tickets can be bought at any travel agency ~~by people / you~~.

✓ ❶ The epic poem "Paradise Lost" was written **by** Milton.
✓ ❷ Tickets can be bought at any travel agency. (**kein by-agent**)

→ Wir können **Passivsätze** mit allen Verben bilden, die im Aktiv ein **Objekt** haben. Weil wir durch die Anwendung des Passivs die Aufmerksamkeit des Lesers auf das Objekt des Aktivsatzes lenken wollen, wird dies zum **Subjekt** des Passivsatzes. Der / die Handelnde – also das Subjekt des Aktivsatzes – kann mit **by** (**nicht** *from)* auch dem Passivsatz angeschlossen werden ❶.
Vergleichen Sie:

Aktiv:	Kate Chopin	**wrote**	"A Shameful Affair".
	Subjekt	**Verb**	**Objekt**
Passiv:	"A Shameful Affair"	**was written**	**by** Kate Chopin.
	Subjekt	**Verb**	**by-agent**

→ Einen **by-agent** verwendet man besonders dann, wenn hervorgehoben werden soll, von wem etwas getan wurde:
Schumann didn't write this sonata. It was written **by Brahms**.
What do you mean "we"? All the real work was done **by Tom**.

→ Beachten Sie aber, dass ein *by-agent* in echten Passivsätzen selten vorkommt. Ein häufiger Fehler ist der überflüssige oder falsche Gebrauch eines *by-agent* bei Wörtern wie **everybody**, **people**, **somebody**, **you** usw. ❷.

Exercise 2 Re-write these active sentences in the passive. Only use a **by**-agent when absolutely necessary.

☀ They started work on the cathedral in 1087.
Work on the cathedral was started in 1087.

1 Steinbeck, not Hemingway, wrote "The Grapes of Wrath".

____

____ .

2 Visitors can buy tickets at the main entrance.

____ .

3 Readers should not take reference books out of the library.

____ .

4 People use computers to process all kinds of data.

____ .

5 They developed the micropchip in the late 1960s.

____ .

6 The University of Pennsylvania built the first modern computer in 1946.

____ .

____ .

7 Very few people support the testing of nuclear weapons.

____ .

8 In case of breakdown, users must inform the manufacturers at once.

____ .

____ .

3 Das unpersönliche Passiv

① ~~It said~~ that Sarah is going to have a baby.
② Alcohol ~~is be thought to be~~ one cause of heart trouble.

✓ ❶ **It is said** that Sarah is going to have a baby.
✓ ❷ Alcohol **is thought to be** one cause of heart trouble.

→ Viele Schüler/innen haben Schwierigkeiten, das unpersönliche Passiv *(impersonal passive)* zu bilden. Beachten Sie daher diese Satzmuster:

It	**is**	**believed**	(that)	…	❶
		claimed			
		said			
		thought			
…	**is**	**believed**	to be	…	❷
	are	**claimed**			
	was	**said**			
	were	**thought**			

Wir benutzen das unpersönliche Passiv, wenn wir eine **Aussage objektiv und neutral** – also eben unpersönlich – ausdrücken wollen. Daher kommt es vor allem in formellen Berichten, Leitartikeln usw. vor.

→ Beachten Sie, dass im Deutschen diese Struktur anders ausgedrückt wird:
It is claimed the Prime Minister will resign soon.
Man behauptet, dass der Premierminister bald zurücktreten wird.
Tourism **is said to be** Britain's second biggest industry.
Angeblich soll Tourismus die zweitgrößte Industrie Britanniens sein.

Exercise 3 Rewrite the sentences using the impersonal passive. Include a **by**-agent when necessary. Study the examples first.

People think that the company will expand.
It is thought that the company will expand.

The survey said that angling is Britain's most popular sport.
Angling is said to be Britain's most popular sport.

1 Some speakers claimed that the crime rate is now falling.

________________________ that the crime rate is now falling.

2 Porn-dealers will say that customers just get what they want.

____ that customers just get what they want.

3 The report found that private cars are serious polluters.

____ serious polluters.

4 A few weird sects believe that the world will end in 2020.

_____________________________________ that the world will end in 2020.

5 They say that middle-class voters are turning to Labour.

______________________________________ turning to Labour.

6 A lot of drug-users say that hashish is less dangerous than alcohol.

________________________________ less dangerous than alcohol.

Exercise 4 Read the report from a British weekly news-magazine on page 83 and fill in the correct verb forms. Some forms are active, some are passive.

Jailbirds

One peculiar thing about Britain ______ *be* the television licence fee. This ____________ *pay* by all television owners whether they ____________ *watch* the BBC or not. One argument against the licence fee ______ *be* that most of the money ________________ *not spend* on making programmes, but on the BBC's huge bureaucracy. But here ______ *be* an argument that you ________________ __________ *probably* + *not hear* : non-payment of the licence fee _______ *be* the reason why 14% of jailed women ______ ___________ *put* behind bars. ______ ___________________ *that fact* / *surprise* you? Then just ____________ *look at* another British oddity: putting citizens in jail. In Britain, punishments ______ *be* harsher than anywhere else in the Union. It __________________ *show*, for example, that British judges __________ *send* seven times more people to jail than their Dutch colleagues ______ *do.* In the early 1980s the prison population __________ *grow* so fast that judges ____________________ *must ask* to be more tolerant. The reason _______ *have* nothing to do with being kind. The fact _______ *be* that Britain _______________ __________ *simply* + *run out* of prisons. Since then, however, more prisons ____________________ *build* and judges ________________ _____ *again* + *start* making enthusiastic use of them. Women ___________ *suffer* more from harsh sentencing for trivial crimes than men. It ____________________ *point out* in a recent report that the number of women in jail ________________ *increase* by 40% since 1993 – and 35% of them ______________________ *lock up* on first conviction. In the case of male prisoners, only 12% ______________ __________ *imprison* on first conviction. One woman whose case _____________ ________ *investigate* by the writers of the report ____________ *jail* for two weeks for not paying her television licence fee. Although the judge ____________ *tell* that the woman's partner ____________ ____________ *recently* + *die* and that she ______ ____________________ *confront* by money problems, she __________ __________ *still* + *send* to prison. Her two small children ___________________ *must take* into care at a cost many times that of a television licence. The judge's argument: "I _______ *be* sorry, but the law _____________________ *must obey* in all circumstances".

adapted from a report in The Economist, 15 - 21 July 1995

B 5 Fehler bei Verb + Verb-Zusammensetzungen

1 Verb + Infinitiv mit *to* oder *-ing*-Form

① Sarah ~~enjoys to go~~ to parties.
② Do you ~~mind not to do~~ that?
③ I ~~hope meet~~ you again soon.

✓ ❶ Sarah **enjoys going** to parties.
✓ ❷ Do you **mind not doing** that?
✓ ❸ I **hope to meet** you again soon.

→ Nach einer Gruppe von Verben folgt immer der **to-Infinitiv**, nach einer anderen Gruppe immer die **-ing-Form**.

→ Der Standardfehler ist, diese beiden Gruppen zu verwechseln, oft wird der Infinitiv zu häufig verwendet ❶, ❷.
Ein weiterer Fehler, der gelegentlich vorkommt, ist, den Infinitiv ohne **to** zu benutzen ❸.

→ Da es keine verlässliche Regel gibt, die die beiden Verbgruppen auf Anhieb bestimmt, bleibt Ihnen nichts anderes übrig, als sich die folgenden Listen zu merken:

Verb + to-Infinitiv

afford	I'm afraid we **can't afford to go** on holiday this year. *(sich leisten)*
choose	You **can choose to leave** home if you want. *(wählen)*
decide	Betty **hasn't decided to take** the job yet. *(entscheiden*
expect	I **expect to see** you all hard at work when I come in. *(erwarten)*
hope	Alison **hopes to get** a place at Cambridge. *(hoffen)*
intend	Carr & Co **intends to open** a factory in the USA. *(beabsichtigen)*
mean	**Do you mean to give up** your job? *(beabsichtigen)*
plan	The town **is planning to build** a new road here. *(planen)*
promise	**Will you promise not to do** such a thing ever again? *(versprechen)*
refuse	Ted **refused to do** overtime this weekend. *(sich weigern)*
try	I **tried to repair** the car, but I couldn't. *(versuchen)*
want	Sally and Greg **want to marry** next spring. *(wollen)*
wish	I don't **wish to disturb** you, but … could you just help me? *(sich wünschen)*

Verb + -ing-Form

admit	Fingers Fred **didn't admit stealing** the money. *(zugeben)*
avoid	You **can't avoid seeing** Tom all the time, Wendy. *(vermeiden)*
consider	**Have you considered asking** a lawyer for advice? *(bedenken)*
deny	She **denied having** anything to do with the crime. *(verneinen)*
dislike	Ann **dislikes working** in London. *(nicht mögen)*
enjoy	I **enjoy going** for long walks in the country. *(genießen)*
finish	They still **haven't finished repairing** our car. *(beenden)*
hate	Ted **hates doing** overtime at the weekend. *(hassen)*
imagine	**Imagine winning** £1m in the national lottery! *(sich vorstellen)*
like	Jane **likes cooking** fabulous meals for her friends. *(mögen)*
love	Mrs Greg **loves working** in her garden. *(sehr mögen)*
mention	Bob **didn't mention meeting** Sue last night. *(erwähnen)*
mind	**Do you mind giving** me a lift home, please? *(irgendetwas dagegen haben)*
miss	We **missed seeing** this film when it first came out. *(versäumen)*
practise	Ann **should practise playing** more difficult music. *(üben)*
prefer	We **prefer staying** at home during the week. *(vorziehen)*
regret	Helen **regrets not going** to university now. *(bedauern)*
risk	Carr & Co **is risking upsetting** the unions. *(riskieren)*
suggest	You **suggested accepting** the price, not me. *(vorschlagen)*

Exercise 1 Put in the right form of the verb.

1 We missed ______________ the band when they played here last year. ↝ *see*

2 I hope ______________ a place at university next year. ↝ *get*

3 Have you considered ______________ your teacher for help? ↝ *ask*

4 Do you mind ______________ that window, please? ↝ *close*

5 The council is planning ______________ more money on schools this year. ↝ *spend*

6 I still haven't finished ______________ the texts for our English class. ↝ *read*

2 Verb + Infinitiv oder *-ing*-Form mit unterschiedlicher Bedeutung

① Do you ~~remember to sit~~ on the beach and ~~to watch~~ the sun go down?
② Don't ~~forget stopping~~ to get some bread.

✓ ❶ Do you **remember sitting** on the beach and **watching** the sun go down?
✓ ❷ Don't **forget to stop** to get some bread.

→ Eine begrenzte Zahl von Verben können je nach Sprecherintention mit dem **to-Infinitiv** oder mit der **-ing-Form** verwendet werden. Am wichtigsten sind:

→ **forget, remember**
Bezieht sich der Satz auf die **Vergangenheit**, nehmen diese beiden Verben die **-ing-Form**. Handelt es sich um die **Zukunft**, stehen die nachfolgenden Verben im **Infinitiv**.

Vergleichen Sie:
I'll never forget meeting my wife for the first time. *(vergessen)*
Don't forget to bring your dictionaries tomorrow. *(vergessen)*
Do you remember visiting Bayeux a few years ago? *(sich erinnern)*
Remember to buy some bread on your way home. *(sich erinnern)*

→ **stop**
Bedeutet **stop** „aufhören, irgend etwas zu tun", steht das angeschlossene Verb in der **-ing-Form**. Wenn aber **stop** „kurz anhalten, um irgend etwas anderes zu tun" bedeutet, dann folgt ein Verb im **Infinitiv**.

Vergleichen Sie:
Ted **must stop working** because of his illness.
Ted muss wegen seiner Krankheit aufhören zu arbeiten.
Why **didn't you stop to ask** the way?
Warum hast du nicht angehalten, um nach dem Weg zu fragen?

Exercise 2 Finish translating the sentences into English.

1 *Vergesst bitte nicht, eure Sportsachen morgen mitzubringen.*

_______________________________ your sports things with you tomorrow.

2 *Keiner kann erwarten, dass eine Frau mit einem gewalttätigen Mann zusammenlebt.*

_______________________________ to live with a violent husband.

3 *Solisten müssen jeden Tag das Singen üben.*

______________________________________ every day.

4 *Die Firma gibt zu, dass sie Waffen in den Irak exportiert hat.*

______________________________________ arms to Iraq.

5 *Der Premierminister hat sich entschlossen, im Herbst eine Wahl einzuberufen.*

____

an election in the autumn.

6 *Ich wünsche mir, dass Bob aufhören würde, solche Lügen zu erzählen.*

I wish __________________________________ such lies.

Exercise 3 Use the **-ing**-form or the **to**-infinitiv.

1 I'm afraid we forgot ________________ you yesterday. *telephone*

2 We can't afford ________________ endless amounts on social security. *spend*

3 My doctor suggested ________________ a check-up in hospital. *have*

4 Sarah stopped ________________ when she had her first child. *work*

5 The defence tried ________________ the jury of their client's innocence. *convince*

6 No tourist should miss ________________ Stonehenge. It's a real must. *visit*

7 The EU is planning ________________ a green tax on heavy lorries. *introduce*

8 Few of us can imagine ________________ our homes and ________________ refugees. *lose, become*

9 I'll never forget ________________ our team's victory in 1996. *celebrate*

B 6 Fehler in if-Sätzen

1 Form

① If Sarah ~~will find~~ a job next year, she won't go to university.
② Jim would buy a house if he ~~would have~~ enough money.
③ If the ambulance had come at once, the patient ~~had not had died~~.

✓ ❶ If Sarah **finds** a job next year, she won't go to university.
✓ ❷ Jim would buy a house if he **had** enough money.
✓ ❸ If the ambulance had come at once, the patient **would not have died**.

→ Ein häufiger Fehler ist die Verwendung von *will / would / would have* im **if**-Teil des Satzes ❶, ❷ bzw. die Verwendung des Past Perfect in beiden Teilen des Satzes bei **if**-Sätzen des Typ III ❸. Auch bei Fragen und der Verneinung kommen manchmal sinnstörende Fehler vor.

→ Die **drei Arten von if-Sätzen** weisen viele verschiedene Kombinationen von Zeiten auf, aber die wichtigsten sind:

Typ I			
If Ann	gets the job, she	will move	to London.
	Simple Present	**will-future**	
Typ II			
If Ann	got the job, she	would move	to London.
	Simple Past	**would Infinitiv**	
Typ III			
If Ann	had got the job, she	would have moved	to London.
	Past Perfect	**would have 3. Form**	

→ Merken Sie sich aber: Je nach Sinn können **andere Modalverben** im **Hauptteil** verwendet werden, z.B.:
If Ann **gets** the job, she **will have to move** to London. –
zwingende Notwendigkeit
If Ann **got** the job, she **could move** to London. –
gute Möglichkeit
If Ann **had got** the job, she **might have moved** to London. –
vage Möglichkeit

→ Beachten Sie, dass bei **Fragen** nur der **Hauptteil** als Frage gebildet wird. Dann steht dieser Teil am Anfang des Satzes:
Would Tony agree to the plan if it cost less?
Würde Tony dem Plan zustimmen, wenn es weniger kostete?
Would Tony have agreed to the plan if it had cost less?
Hätte Tony dem Plan zugestimmt, wenn es weniger gekostet hätte?

→ Je nach Sinn können wir den **if-Teil**, den **Hauptteil** oder **beide Teile** eines **if**-Satzes **verneinen**:

if-Teil: If Ben **doesn't get** the job, he will move to London.
Wenn Ben die Stelle nicht bekommt, zieht er nach London.

Hauptteil: If Ben gets the job, he **won't move** to London.
Wenn Ben die Stelle bekommt, zieht er nicht nach London.

beide Teile: If Ben **doesn't get** the job, he **won't move** to London.
Wenn Ben die Stelle nicht bekommt, zieht er nicht nach London.

Exercise 1 Fill in the correct form of the verbs. Use the type of **if**-sentence – **I, II** or **III** – given. Be careful about negatives.

1 If the Tories ____________ the election, it ____________ their fifth successive victory. ↝ **I:** *win, be*

2 If politicians ____________ money more wisely, people ____________ ____________ willing to pay higher taxes. ↝ **II:** *spend, be*

3 The chairman ____________________ if this year's results ____________ better. ↝ **I:** *must + go, not be*

4 The Asian youths ____________________________ if the police ______________ more sense. ↝ **III:** *riot, show*

5 The Ulster peace talks __________________ immediately if London ______________ its demand for total disarmament.
↝ **II:** *start, abandon*

6 A lot of Tories __________________________ the Treaty of Rome if they ______________________ all the implications.
↝ **III:** *not sign, understand*

Exercise 2 Complete the **if**-sentence questions.

1 ____ the report if it is unfavourable? ↝ *the government / publish*

2 ____ if NATO had acted more decisively? ↝ *the crisis / spread*

3 ______________________________ the EU if the other members were willing? ↝ *Russia / join*

4 ______________________________ the election if the economy goes on improving? ↝ *Labour / win*

5 ______________________________ welfare spending if they were in office? ↝ *the Republicans / cut*

6 ______________________________ so quickly if everyone had known the full cost? ↝ *Germany / reunite*

2 Gebrauch

① If I ~~won~~ a lot of money, I'll stop working.
② If I ~~win~~ a lot of money, I'd stop working.
③ If Fred ~~wasn't late~~ yesterday, Mr Green wouldn't have been angry with him.

✓ ❶ If I **win** a lot of money, I will stop working.
✓ ❷ If I **won** a lot of money I'd stop working.
✓ ❸ If Fred **hadn't been** late yesterday, Mr Green wouldn't have been angry with him.

→ Was den **Gebrauch von if-Sätzen** angeht, haben wir die folgenden Fehler immer wieder festgestellt:
Die Anwendung einer Mischung aus Typ I und Typ II für eine (sehr) wahrscheinliche zukünftige Folge ❶, ❷ und die Anwendung einer Mischung aus Typ II und Typ III für eine unmögliche Folge ❸.

→ Die **drei Typen von if-Sätzen** unterscheiden sich gemäß der **Wahrscheinlichkeit** der zu erwartenden Folge:

Typ I
Die Folge ist **sicher** oder sehr **wahrscheinlich**:
If the government **introduces** the new tax, it **will lose** the election.
Sinn: *Die Regierung wird sicherlich die Wahl verlieren.*

Typ II
Die Folge ist **theoretisch möglich**, aber (sehr) **unwahrscheinlich**:
If Britain **left** the EU it **would become** completely isolated.
Sinn: *Es ist fast undenkbar, dass Großbritannien die EU verlässt.*

Typ III
Die Folge ist **unmöglich**, da wir das Ergebnis schon kennen:
If the EU **had introduced** a single currency in 1995, there **would have been** chaos.
Sinn: *Der Sprecher weiß schon, dass die EU dieses nicht getan hat.*

Exercise 3 Complete the sentences. Read the German first to find out which type of **if**-sentence you should use.

☀ *Es ist äußerst unwahrscheinlich, dass die Regierung strengere Gesetze einführen wird.*

Women's rights **will not improve** if there **are** no stricter anti-discrimination laws. ↝ *not improve; be*

1 *Es ist sicher, dass diese Situation zu Stande kommen wird.*

We ________________ the house if Jack ________________ a job soon.

↝ *must + sell; not find*

2 *Wir wissen schon, dass Deutschland sehr schnell gehandelt hat.*

If Germany ________________ quickly, it ________________ ________________ the chance of reunifying. ↝ *not act; miss*

3 *Eine Erhöhung der Beiträge wird sicherlich die genannte Folge haben.*

If the unions ________________ membership fees, they ________________ even more members. ↝ *increase; lose*

4 *Es ist kaum vorstellbar, dass mehr Geld in die Schulen investiert wird.*

The schools crisis ________________ solved if more money ________________ invested in education. ↝ *be; be*

5 *Es ist sicherlich der Fall, dass die Folge eintreten wird.*

If we ________________ car ownership, our roads ________ ________________ impossible to use. ↝ *not restict; become*

6 *Die Franzosen werden mit aller Wahrscheinlichkeit weiterhin eine Autobahngebühr erheben.*

If the French ________________ road tolls, the country ________________ such wonderful motorways.

↝ *not charge; not have*

7 *Wir wissen, dass die Republikaner die Wahl gewonnen haben.*

The Republicans ________________ the elections if more people ________________ . ↝ *not win; vote*

B 7 Fehler in Relativsätzen

1 Relativpronomen

① Sarah is the girl ~~which~~ told me your name.
② Are those the boys ~~to who~~ you spoke?
③ Sally is the girl ~~who~~ boyfriend is German.

✓ ❶ Sarah is the girl **who / that** told me your name.
✓ ❷ Are those the boys **to whom** you spoke?
✓ ❸ Sally is the girl **whose** boyfriend is German.

→ Für deutschsprachige Lernende sind englische Relativsätze wenig problematisch. Folgende Fehler treten auf:
which statt **who** für Personen ❶,
who statt **whom** nach Präpositionen ❷,
who anstelle der besitzanzeigenden Form **whose** ❸.

→ Für Personen benutzen wir **who** / **that** ❶ und für Dinge **which** / **that**. Diese Pronomen haben immer dieselbe Form. Hier sind zwei weitere Beispiele:
A novel **which** / **that** shocked the American conscience was "The Grapes of Wrath".
John Steinbeck was an author **who** / **that** wrote about social problems.

→ Beachten Sie: Ist das Relativpronomen das **Objekt** des Relativsatzes, können wir es **weglassen**:
The novel (which / that) we read last year was "Lord of the Flies".
The characters (who / that) the novel is about are schoolboys.

Relativsätze **ohne** zwingende Relativpronomen nennen wir **Contact Clauses**.

→ Bei Personen wird grundsätzlich **whom** – nicht *who* / *that* – nach Präpositionen verwendet ❷:
Is Mrs Carr the woman **for whom** you bought the present?
The family **with whom** I stayed were charming.

→ Bei Sachen benutzen wir nach Präpositionen **which**:
This is the poster **for which** Ann paid over £1,000.
Is this the special key **with which** you turn on the computer?

→ Um Besitz anzuzeigen, verwenden wir **whose** bei Personen und Sachen. Dieses Pronomen hat ebenfalls immer dieselbe Form ❸:
Susan Hall is the journalist **whose reports** caused so much trouble.
The party **whose voters** stay at home will lose the election.

Exercise 1 Fill in **who, which, whom** or **whose**.

1 This is the article to ______________ I referred in my essay.

2 The character ______________ girlfriend left him is called Carles Lumley.

3 The paper ______________ published the report is the Guardian.

4 The woman to ______________ I was just talking is my boss's wife.

5 Is that the family ______________ children you teach?

6 People ______________ don't pay their taxes are no better than thieves.

Exercise 2 Form past tense sentences with the elements. Add any additional words and use a relative pronoun only when necessary.

affirmative action / be / policy / give / special help / blacks
Affirmative action was a policy that gave special help to blacks.

1 policy / help / blacks / get / employment / be / once / just / whites
The policy helped blacks ______________________________________
______________________________________ .

2 it / grow / popular support / people / give / Civil Rights Movement
It grew from the ______________________________________
______________ Civil Rights Movement.

3 this / be / movement / be led / Martin Luther King
This was the movement ______________________________________
______________ .

4 Lyndon Johnson / be / president / make / affirmative action / law
Lyndon Johnson was ______________________________________
affirmative action law.

5 it / be / policy / always / cause / great deal / argument
It was ______________________________________
______________________________ .

6 there / be / Republicans / believe / it / be / undemocratic
There were ______________________________________
______________________________________ .

2 Notwendige und nicht-notwendige Relativsätze

① Elvis Presley, ~~that~~ died in 1977, was a famous pop-singer.
② The ferry, that sank, was on its way to Helsinki.
③ The girl, who got the job, is the boss's daughter.

✓ ❶ Elvis Presley, **who** died in 1977, was a famous pop-singer.
✓ ❷ The ferry that sank was on its way to Helsinki. (**keine** Kommata)
✓ ❸ The girl who got the job is the boss's daughter. (**keine** Kommata)

→ Wir unterscheiden zwischen Informationen, die für die Satzbedeutung notwendig sind und Informationen, die entbehrlich sind.
Können wir die Bedeutung des Hauptsatzes nur an Hand der Zusatzinformation im Relativsatz verstehen, dann handelt es sich um einen **notwendigen** *(defining)* **Relativsatz** ❷, ❸.
Können wir aber den Hauptsatz **ohne** den Relativsatz verstehen, dann haben wir es mit einem **nicht-notwendigen** *(non-defining)* **Relativsatz** zu tun ❶.

→ Sehen Sie sich die Beispiele oben genauer an:
Im Falle von **Satz 1** können wir den Hauptsatz **ohne** die Information **who died in 1977** gut verstehen.
Bei **Satz 2** und **Satz 3** dagegen können wir die Hauptsätze nur mit Hilfe der zusätzlichen Informationen **that sank** ❷ und **who got the job** ❸ richtig verstehen.

→ Beachten Sie, dass bei **nicht-notwendigen Relativsätzen** ❶ wir **who** für Personen und **which** für Sachen benutzen. Die Alternative *that* ist **nicht** möglich.

→ Da bei **notwendigen Relativsätzen** die hinzugefügten Informationen unentbehrlich sind, verwenden wir **keine Kommata**, um den Relativsatz vom Hauptsatz zu trennen ❷, ❸.

→ Der untergeordnete Stellenwert eines **nicht-notwendigen Relativsatzes** dagegen wird signalisiert, indem wir ihn zwischen **Kommata** setzen.
Hier sind ein paar weitere Beispiele:

nicht-notwendig:	John F. Kennedy, **whose family came from Ireland,** was shot in Dallas.
notwendig:	The woman **whose husband died in the accident** lives in our road.
nicht-notwendig:	The car, **which was a red Golf,** had been stolen the day before.
notwendig:	The car **which / that was stolen by the thieves** belongs to a policeman.

Exercise 3 Use arrows to put the relative clauses in brackets into the sentences. Include commas where the clauses are non-defining.

1 A survey was presented to the home secretary yesterday.
(that investigates sexual equality in Britain)

2 The survey found that little has changed.
(which was published in the *Guardian*)

3 The results make sad reading for women.
(which come from all over the UK)

4 It was found that in Britain today it is still women.
(who do most household jobs)

5 This applied to working women as well.
(who themselves have jobs)

6 The survey showed that even young men do not help much in the home.
(who are out of work)

7 While it was men, women had to do all the routine jobs.
(who did household repairs)

8 Isobel Hall says couples should discuss the division of work honestly.
(who is a sociologist at London University)

9 Above all, women should not be automatically and unfairly disadvantaged.
(who now make up nearly 50% of the workforce)

10 English law at least makes equality at work a legal requirement.
(which was only recently changed)

11 Equality is something but we have got a long way to go before it is reality.
(which we are aiming at)

B 8 Weitere Fehler mit der -ing-Form

1 Die *-ing*-Form nach Präpositionen und Redewendungen

① Caroline joined the animal rights movement ~~after see~~ a report on TV.
② We ~~are looking forward to go~~ on holiday.
③ It's ~~no good to ask~~ Mr Grubb for help.

❶ Caroline joined the animal rights movement **after seeing** a report on TV. ✓
❷ We **are looking forward to going** on holiday. ✓
❸ It's **no good asking** Mr Grubb for help. ✓

→ Hier ist der Fehler leicht zu erkennen. Viele Schüler tendieren dazu, den Infinitiv – mit oder ohne *to* – statt der -ing-Form nach Präpositionen ❶, ❷ und nach einigen festen Redewendungen, wie z.B. **it's no good** ❸, zu verwenden.
Merken Sie sich daher, dass wir **immer** die **-ing-Form** nach **Präpositionen** gebrauchen. Dies gilt nicht nur für Präpositionen, die alleine stehen ❶, sondern auch für Zusammensetzungen aus
- **Verb + Präposition** ❷,
- **Substantiv + Präposition** und
- **Adjektiv + Präposition**.

→ Beachten Sie auch, dass die folgenden **Redewendungen** ebenfalls die **-ing-Form** nehmen:
It's no good thinking I'll change my mind. *(es hat keinen Zweck)*
It's no use having the camera repaired. *(es hat keinen Sinn)*
I don't think **it's worth** going to that film. *(es lohnt sich)*
It's not worth doing overtime nowadays. *(es lohnt sich nicht)*
How about eating out this evening? *(wie wäre es mit …?)*
What about inviting Jill for a beer? *(wie wäre es mit …?)*
Syd is dishonest **as well as** being lazy. *(sowohl als auch)*
Do something useful, **like** cutting the grass, for example. *(wie [zum Beispiel])*
Can you do something to help, **such as** opening the wine? *(wie [zum Beispiel])*
There's nothing I like more **than** having a good read. *(als)*

Exercise 1 Make sentences from the elements. Use the given tense and add any missing articles, prepositions etc. Study the examples first.

manager / be sacked / for + take bribes → *simple past*
The manager **was sacked for taking bribes.**

you / only + can use / this barbecue / for + cook / outside → *simple present*
You can only use this barbecue **for cooking** outside.

1 Sally / fail / exam / in spite of + have / a lot / private lessons
simple past

Sally ____

________________________ private lessons.

2 be no good + expect / me / live / your life / you *simple present*

____

____________________ you.

3 instead of + work / Jane / spend / her time / dream / of + become / actress *simple past*

____ her

time _________________________________ actress.

4 there be / no alternative / to + learn / these idioms / heart
simple present

_____________ no alternative _________________ these

idioms _____________ .

5 our teacher / never + give / us / chance / of + discuss /
our own ideas *present perfect*

Our teacher ___________________________________

____________________ our own ideas.

6 Sarah / recently + succeed / in + sell / several / her paintings
present perfect

Sarah ____

__________________ her paintings.

7 it / not be worth + repair / our old car / again *will-future*

____

___________ our old car again.

8 we / look forward to + receive / your answer / shortly

present progressive

We ____

your answer shortly.

9 you / never + train / your dog / by + hit / him *will-future*

You ____

____________ him.

2 Die *-ing*-Form als Substantiv

① ~~To smoke~~ is bad for you.
② Jim goes ~~to ski~~ every year.
③ The British are helping with ~~the rebuild~~ of Dresden.

✓ ❶ **Smoking** is bad for you.
✓ ❷ Jim goes **skiing** every year.
✓ ❸ The British are helping with **the rebuilding** of Dresden.

→ Bei dem Gebrauch der **-ing-Form** als Substantiv (Gerund) ist der Standardfehler die Verwendung des Infinitivs statt der **-ing-Form** ❶ – ❸. Merken Sie sich: Wenn wir ein Verb als Substantiv verwenden, dann benutzen wir die **-ing-Form** in genau derselben Art und Weise wie jedes andere Substantiv, z.B.:

Subjekt: **Cycling is becoming** increasingly popular.
Rad fahren wird zunehmend beliebter.

Objekt: A lot of doctors **recommend swimming** to their patients.
Viele Ärzte empfehlen ihren Patienten das Schwimmen.

Nach Artikeln: **The rebuilding** of Dresden will take ages.
Der Wiederaufbau Dresdens wird ewig dauern.

Mit Adjektiven: For heaven's sake stop this **awful arguing**.
Um Himmels Willen hört mit dieser fürchterlichen Streiterei auf.

Exercise 2 Finish translating the sentences into English. Use the **-ing**-form.

1 *Viele Leute haben Angst vor dem Fliegen.*

A lot of people ______________________________ .

2 *Leider hat er keine Erfahrung im Unterrichten von Erwachsenen.*

Unfortunately, ______________________________

______________ adults.

3 *Sie können Menschen nicht daran hindern zu denken.*

You can't prevent ______________________________ .

4 *Mein Tag bestand aus dem Zuhören von endlosen Reden.*

My day ______________________________ .

5 *Ich bin nicht daran gewöhnt, so unhöflich angesprochen zu werden.*

I am not used ______________________________ .

6 *Die Dozentin fing damit an, uns zu erzählen, wie schlau sie sei.*

The lecturer ______________________________

______________________ .

Exercise 3 This extract from a love story is an example of "light romantic literature". Read the story and complete it with verbs from the list. There are plenty of clues that will help you find the right verb, for example **read a letter**. Use the **-ing**-form throughout.

beat, be caught, come, fight, go about, hold, kiss, light, listen, look, look around, look at, open, pass, pick up, plead [*flehen*], read, remove, smoke, take, turn, wait, whisper

The Complete Love Story

On ______________ Michael's letter, Lisa was sick with pain. At first she felt like ______________ the phone and ______________ with him to change his mind. But with the ______________ of the hours she realized that there was no use ______________ for him. She had lost. The other woman had won. ______________ for the man she loved, ______________ to his tender voice whispering sweet words in her ear, ______________ deep into his loving eyes – all that was over, a thing of the past.

______________ the gun in her hand, Lisa asked herself what he would say when he heard of her suicide. Would he feel guilty? Would he weep? Slowly she put the gun to her forehead.

But weren't there steps outside on the garden path? His steps? ______________ to her door?

Lisa heard a key __________________ in the lock and – as if in a dream – saw the door __________________ . Then, with a little cry of delight, she was in Michael's arms, her heart __________________ loudly, still __________________ the gun between her fingers.
__________________ Lisa's lips tenderly, Michael got the gun out of her hand. And then he fired. __________________ his name, Lisa sank to the floor – she was dead.

__________________ the gun from the handkerchief in which he was holding it, Michael pressed it into Lisa's hand. After __________________ the room for a last time, he left. A few seconds later he was out of the house in the street. Everybody was busy __________________ their business. Nobody seemed to notice him.

Michael was still weeping bitter tears at Lisa's grave when Inspector Radley said to him: "Michael Webb, I am arresting you for the murder of Lisa Sutton."
__________________ the inspector in horror, Michael tried to think. How could the police know? Hadn't he arranged everything so carefully that there was no risk of __________________ ?

As they were driving to the police station, Radley took out some cigarettes.
__________________ one himself, he offered the packet to Michael.
"Care for a cigarette?" the inspector asked. "You do smoke, don't you?"
Then Michael knew. The cigarette end in the ashtray on the table in Lisa's sitting room. His favourite brand, Pegasus Kingsize. Everybody knew that Lisa had never gone in for __________________ .

B 9 Fehler bei der indirekten Rede

1 Allgemeine Bemerkungen

① The author ~~writes that~~ Charles ~~wanted~~ to get drunk.
② In the first scene Rita ~~told~~ the professor that she ~~is~~ dissatisfied with her life.
③ The survey ~~found that~~ most voters ~~expected~~ politicians to lie.
④ Phil ~~says his friends / tells~~ that he is bored.
⑤ Jody tells ~~him~~ that he does not think ~~he will~~ care.

✓ ❶ The author **writes that** Charles **wants** to get drunk.
✓ ❷ In the first scene Rita **told** the professor that she **was** dissatisfied with her life.
✓ ❸ The survey **found** that most voters **expect** polticians to lie.
✓ ❹ Phil **says** (**to his friends**) / **tells his friends** that he is bored.
✓ ❺ Jody tells **Billy** that he does not think **his father** will care.

Im Zusammenhang mit der **indirekten Rede** sind die häufigsten Fehler:

→ Die unzulässige Anwendung der Zeitverschiebung, wenn das einleitende Verb im Präsens steht ❶. Der Grund dieses Fehlers liegt darin, dass in der Oberstufe die indirekte Rede oft in Form von Zitaten vorkommt. Da wir aber das **Präsens** benutzen, um über Texte zu reden, bleibt die **Zeitfolge unverändert**.

→ Die Auslassung der Zeitverschiebung, wenn das einleitende Verb in der **Vergangenheit** steht ❷. Steht das einleitende Verb in der Vergangenheit (**said**, **told**, **wondered** usw.), dann werden alle Zeiten **eine Zeitstufe zurück** in die Vergangenheit versetzt, außer, wenn es sich um eine noch geltende Situation handelt ❸.

Die Modalverben **can**, **may** und **must** werden in der indirekten Rede als **could**, **might** und **had to** wiedergeben:
SENATOR "We **cannot be expected** to feed half the world."
A senator said the USA **could not be expected** to feed half the world.

→ Merken Sie sich, dass die Zeitverschiebung **nicht** gilt, wenn es sich **zur Zeit der indirekten Äußerung** um noch geltende Situationen ❸, um feste Gewohnheiten oder Ansichten und um Gesetzmäßigkeiten handelt.

→ Fehler im Zusammenhang mit **say** und **tell** als einleitende Verben ❹. Normalerweise wird **say** in der indirekten Rede ohne ein indirektes Objekt benutzt. Wollen wir aber verdeutlichen, wer angesprochen wird, müssen wir **to** gebrauchen. Vergleichen Sie:

ohne indirektes Objekt:	The pilot **said** (that) the plane was late.
mit indirektem Objekt:	The pilot **said to the passengers** (that) the plane was late.

Im Gegensatz zu **say**, haben die Verben **tell** *(mitteilen)* und **inform** ein indirektes Objekt **ohne** *to.*
Das Objekt wird also **direkt angeschlossen**:
The pilot **told the passengers** (that) the plane was late.
The pilot **informed the passengers** (that) the plane was late.

Für Hinweise über weitere einleitende Verben siehe Seite 104.

→ Ein weiterer Fehler ist der sinnentstellende Gebrauch von Pronomen statt Namen bzw. Substantiven ❺.
In der indirekten Rede ist es notwendig, **Personenangaben** aus der Sicht des Berichtenden anzugeben, z.B.:

direkte Rede: MRS HART AT PRESS CONFERENCE "I have talked to the Prime Minister and he has advised me to retire from politics immediately."

indirekte Rede: Mrs Hart told **journalists** that **she** had talked to the Prime Minister and **he** had advised **her** to retire from politics immediately.

Manchmal müssen auch **Namen ergänzt** werden, damit deutlich wird, wer gemeint ist:

direkte Rede: MRS HART "Betty, I have seen Margaret and she wants me to discuss the question with you and then to get back to her as soon as possible."

indirekte Rede: Mrs Hart said that she had seen Margaret and **Margaret** wanted **her** to discuss the question with **Betty** and then get back to **her** as soon as possible.

Exercise 1 Rewrite these statements for a newspaper article using reported speech.

1 MINISTER "The government will take every possible step to ensure that consumption of beef is safe for our children."

The minister said that ______________________________

______________________________ .

2 DOCTOR PROWSE "We have discovered that the disease has occured in more areas than we thought."

Doctor Prowse said that ______________________________

____

______________________________ .

3 JOAN FRENCH "I think the current situation has been made worse by the press who didn't inform the population properly."

Joan French told the press that ______________________________

______________________________ .

4 AMY GARDNER "We don't eat beef in our family and we haven't done for years. I am quite sure that nothing will happen to my family."

Amy Gardner said that ______________________________

____

____ .

5 ALEX BUTCHER "I like beef and I will continue eating it. What's going on is just one big media hype."

Alex Butcher told us that ____________________________

____ .

2 Zwei Fehler mit Fragen

① Susan asked when ~~do~~ ozone layers rise most sharply?
② Susan asked ~~do~~ ozone levels rise more sharply in hot weather?

✓ ❶ Susan asked **when ozone layers rise** most sharply.
✓ ❷ Susan asked **if / whether ozone layers rise** more sharply in hot weather.

→ Enthält die direkte Frage ein **Fragewort**, wird es verwendet, um die indirekte Frage zu bilden ❶.
Gibt es aber **kein Fragewort**, dann benutzen wir **if** bzw. **whether** *(ob)*, um zu verdeutlichen, dass es sich um eine Entscheidungsfrage handelt ❷.
Beachten Sie, dass in beiden Fällen die **Wortstellung** wie bei einem **Aussagesatz** ist. Deshalb benutzen wir **kein Fragezeichen** nach indirekten Fragen.

Exercise 2 Some pupils are asking a visitor from the United Nations Association about the organization. Report the pupils' questions.

☀ "When was the UN founded?" Ann asked **when the UN was founded**.

1 "What is the role of the security council?"

Helen wanted to know ______________________________

______________________ .

2 "How many members had the UN in the beginning?"

Tony asked ______________________________________

in the beginning.

3 "Which countries are permanent members of the security council?"
Jane asked ______________________ permanent members of the security council.

4 "Where was the headquarters of the UN before it moved to New York?"
Mike enquired ____________________________________
____________________________________ to New York.

5 "Does the director-general have to come from a neutral country?"
Chris asked if / whether ______________________________
__________ from a neutral country.

6 "Has the UN lost any influence since the cold war?"
Sarah wanted to know ______________________________
__________________ since the cold war.

3 Einleitende Verben

① The trainer ~~congratulated on winning~~ the match.
② The doctor ~~advised to stop~~ smoking.
③ Mrs Adams ~~reminded to bring~~ our dictionaries to the next lesson.

✓ ❶ The trainer **congratulated the team for / on** winning the match.
✓ ❷ The doctor **advised his patient to stop** smoking.
✓ ❸ Mrs Adams **reminded us to bring** dictionaries to the next lesson.

→ Die **häufigsten einleitenden Verben** sind:

Aussagen: **says, tell**	The writer **says** there is a connection between poverty and crime. In the final sentence we **are told** who Billy really is.
Fragen: **ask**	The leader **asks** if the environment is as endangered as some claim.
Aufforderungen: **tell, ask**	Beatrice **tells** Benedict to kill his friend Claudio. Henry is so hurt that he **asks** Julia to return his ring.

→ Es gibt jedoch eine Reihe von anderen einleitenden Verben, die wir benutzen können, um die Intention des Sprechers genauer wiederzugeben. Viele Fehler sind auf die **Besonderheiten** dieser Verben hinsichtlich des Anschlusses von Objekten zurückzuführen ❶, ❷, ❸.
(Alle folgenden Sätze beziehen sich übrigens auf Shakespeares „Much Ado About Nothing")

Aussagen:

In the end Benedict **believes** that Beatrice loves him. *(glauben)*
Leonato **blames** Hero **for** shaming his family. *(die Schuld geben)*
Don John **accuses** Hero **of** making love to Borachio. *(beschuldigen)*
Leonato **agrees** that Hero has done wrong. *(zustimmen)*
Hero **answers** / **replies** that she has been falsely accused. *(antworten)*
Beatrice **argues** that it is all an awful plot. *(argumentieren)*
The Friar **claims** that Hero is innocent. *(behaupten)*
They **congratulate** him **for** / **on** catching Don John. *(gratulieren)*
Beatrice **doubts** that Benedict is willing to marry. *(bezweifeln)*
He **explains** to Leonato how Hero was wronged. *(erklären)*
Dogberry **informs** Leonato **of** Don John's arrest. *(informieren)*
Don Pedro **points out** that he himself saw Hero. *(hinweisen auf)*
Antonio **reminds** his brother **of** Don John's past. *(erinnern an)*
Dogberry **reports** that he has arrested Don John. *(berichten)*
The Friar **suggests** hiding Hero in a nunnery. *(vorschlagen)*
Friar Francis **thinks** that Hero is definitely innocent. *(meinen)*

Fragen:

Al **enquires** of the servant where Don Pedro is. *(sich erkundigen)*
Beatrice **wants to know** if Benedict is coming, too. *(wissen wollen)*
The judge **wonders** what Dogberry is trying to say. *(sich fragen)*

Aufforderungen, Bitten:

Friar Francis **advises** Leonato to show mercy. *(beraten)*
Hero **pleads with** / **begs** Al to believe her. *(ernsthaft bitten, flehen)*
Don Pedro **commands** Dogberry to arrest them. *(befehlen)*
Leonato **invites** Don Pedro to stay as long as he likes. *(einladen)*
The judge **orders** the prisoners to be brought to him. *(befehlen)*

Exercise 4 Find a suitable verb from the list above. Be careful about tenses.

1 Mr Hudd ________________ the party of ignoring green issues. ⇝ *beschuldigte*

2 The spokeswoman ______________ that the unions will agree to a pay freeze. ⇝ *bezweifelt*

3 Mrs Day ________________ whether the West really supported Serbia. ⇝ *fragte sich*

4 In his book, Forsyth ______________ that the Coalition wanted Saddam Hussein to stay in power. ⇝ *argumentiert*

5 The German health ministers ________________ consumers not to eat British beef. ⇝ *beraten*

6 He _______________ with her not to leave him. ⇝ *flehte*

B 10 Fehler mit gängigen präpositionalen Zusammensetzungen

1 Verb + Präposition-Verbindungen

① We ~~waited on~~ the train for over an hour.
② The man ~~confessed for~~ taking the money.
③ The teacher ~~insisted in~~ silence during the exam.

✓ ❶ We **waited for** the train for over an hour.
✓ ❷ The man **confessed to** taking the money.
✓ ❸ The teacher **insisted on** silence during the exam.

→ Was die Fehleranalyse angeht, liegt die falsche Anwendung von **Präpositionen** und **Partikeln** – siehe auch **B 11** – an der Spitze. Nach dem Grund braucht man nicht lange zu suchen. Der Gebrauch von Präpositionen ist extrem idiomatisch und kann nicht in irgendeinem „Regelwerk" untergebracht werden. Daher kann man nicht oft genug sagen:
Lernen Sie **Präpositionen immer als Teil einer Redewendung**.
Präpositionen als einzelne Wörter zu lernen, hat wenig Zweck, weil sie je nach Kontext viele unterschiedliche Bedeutungen haben. Nehmen wir zum Beispiel die Präposition **at**. Sehen Sie sich die Liste an. Überlegen Sie, wie viele deutsche Bedeutungen **at** hat – und ob es möglich ist, irgendwelche Regel oder gar „Muster" zu erkennen.

at the station *(am Bahnhof)*
at the baker's *(beim Bäcker)*
at the chemist's *(in der Apotheke)*
at my parents' *(bei meinen Eltern)*
at Jim's party *(auf Jims Party)*
at Christmas *(zu Weihnachten)*
at 40 *(mit 40)*
at 6 o'clock *(um 6 Uhr)*
at £3.75 *(für £3.75)*
at last *(endlich)*
be at it *(immer noch dabei sein)*

→ Viele **Präpositionen** kommen in fester **Verbindung mit Verben** vor. Bei diesem Verzeichnis handelt es sich um die gängigsten Wendungen *prepositional verbs*, die in der Oberstufe eine **absolute Voraussetzung** sind:

We **arrived at** the airport late. *(ankommen)*
Can you **ask** the waiter **for** the menu? *(bitten um)*
This car **belongs to** my son. *(gehören)*
Bob **borrowed** £20 **from** me last week. *(ausleihen von)*
Get a job. Don't just **dream about** winning the lottery. *(träumen von)*
Do you **know about** the robbery, Fingers? *(wissen über)*
The children all **laughed at** the teacher. *(auslachen)*
You shouldn't **laugh about** such sad things. *(auslachen)*
This isn't my CD. Sally **lent** it **to** me. *(leihen)*
We **listened to** a Mozart symphony at school today. *(zuhören)*
Look at that man. He hasn't got any shoes on. *(anschauen)*

Did you **read about** that accident in the paper yesterday? *(lesen über)*
I don't know which party to **vote for**. They're all the same. *(wählen)*
Wait for me in the car park, all right? *(warten auf)*
Close your eyes and **wish for** three things. *(sich etwas wünschen)*
James Hardy usually **writes about** politics. *(schreiben über)*
I really must **write to** my mother this weekend. *(schreiben an)*

Exercise 1 Complete the sentences with the correct preposition.

1 There is no point in asking __for_____ more pay in today's economic climate.
2 We are still waiting __for_____ a reply to our letter of 10 August.
3 Banks only lend __to_____ people with security.
4 I find people who laugh __about_____ serious things boring.
5 Most people wish __for_____ good health above all else.
6 Don't just dream __about_____ success – do something to achieve it.

Exercise 2 Complete the sentences with the correct verb. Only one solution is possible. If you are not sure look up the verbs in a dictionary.

1 British and American English ____________ from each other mainly in pronunciation.
2 There's no point in making agreements with people who can't be ____________ on.
3 The Florida tourist board ____________ tourists against going to the poorer areas of Miami.
4 You can't blame non-smokers for ____________ to people smoking in restaurants.
5 Do Hindus ____________ in the resurrection of the spirit or only in reincarnation?
6 Few people believed that Washington would ____________ in defeating the British.
7 It's strange that most experts ____________ of the legalization of drugs.

advises, approve, believe, differ, objecting, relied, succeed

2 Substantiv + Präposition-Verbindungen

① We can't go climbing because of Greg's ~~fear for~~ heights.
② Fred is in trouble because of his ~~lateness at~~ work.
③ Mary's ~~marriage with~~ Tom isn't very happy.

✓ ❶ We can't go climbing because of Greg's **fear of** heights.
✓ ❷ Fred is in trouble because of his **lateness for** work.
✓ ❸ Mary's **marriage to** Tom isn't very happy.

→ Genau wie **Präpositionen** in fester Verbindung mit Verben auftreten, so kommen sie auch **in Verbindung mit Substantiven** *(prepositional nouns)* vor:
I can't hide my **amazement at** his behaviour. *(Erstaunen über)*
She has no **awareness of** the situation of the poor. *(Bewusstsein von)*
Steve has no **interest in** his work at all. *(Interesse an)*
I've paid her. I've no **obligation to** her now. *(Verpflichtung gegenüber)*
Americans feel **shame at** what happened to the Indians. *(Scham für)*
She expressed her **gratitude to** me **for** my help. *(Dankbarkeit jdm. gegenüber für etwas)*

Exercise 3 Use an English prepositional noun for the German expressions. If necessary, look them up in a dictionary.

1 Drugs like morphine have given us virtual ______________ pain.
  ↝ *Freiheit von*
2 The West has little ______________ helping the Third World to industrialize. ↝ *Interesse für (an)*
3 Some people live in ______________ what others think of them. ↝ *Angst über (vor)*
4 Few governments show any real ______________ ordinary people's problems. ↝ *Bewusstsein von*
5 The audience showed its ______________ the ten-year-old girl's talent. ↝ *Erstaunen über*
6 I've got a lot of ______________ my health.
  ↝ *Sorge um*
7 ______________ animals is said to be a very British thing.
  ↝ *Freundlichkeit gegenüber*
8 Brian has changed completely since his ______________ Sally.
  ↝ *Ehe mit*

3 Andere gängige Wendungen mit Präpositionen

① Simon's no loss. He was ~~useless on~~ any case.
② Let's go to the cinema ~~to a change~~.

✓ ❶ Simon's no loss. He was useless **in any case**.
✓ ❷ Let's go to the cinema **for a change**.

→ Dieses Verzeichnis beinhaltet die wichtigsten **Wendungen mit Präpositionen** *(prepositional phrases)*. Auch hier bleibt Ihnen nichts anderes übrig, als die Wendungen auswendig zu lernen:

at best / worst *(bestenfalls / schlimmstenfalls)*
at first sight *(auf den ersten Blick)*
at leisure *(in Ruhe)*
at length *(ausführlich)*

by accident *(versehentlich)*
by chance *(zufällig)*
by hand *(mit der Hand)*
by heart *(auswendig)*
by means of *(mit Hilfe von)*
by mistake *(versehentlich)*
by the way *(übrigens)*
by virtue of *(auf Grund)*

for a change *(zur Abwechslung)*
for better or for worse *(„was immer daraus werden wird")*

from bad to worse *(immer schlechter)*
from now on *(von jetzt an)*
from then on *(seitdem)*

in addition to *(zusätzlich)*
in any case / event *(jedenfalls)*
in case of *(für den Fall, dass)*
in comparison with *(im Vergleich zu)*
in contrast to *(im Gegensatz zu)*
in depth *(gründlich)*
in detail *(Punkt für Punkt)*
in general *(im Allgemeinen)*
in practice *(in der Praxis)*
in theory *(theoretisch)*
in / **under** the circumstances *(unter den gegebenen Umständen)*
in view of *(angesichts)*

off the map *(nicht auf der Karte)*
off the record *(im Vertrauen)*

on average *(durchschnittlich)*
on behalf of *(im Namen von)*
on foot *(zu Fuß)*
on no account *(auf keinen Fall)*
on purpose *(absichtlich)*
on the contrary *(im Gegenteil)*
on time *(zeitig)*

out of character *(untypisch)*
out of date / fashion *(unzeitgemäß, altmodisch)*
out of favour *(unbeliebt)*
out of hand *(außer Kontrolle)*
out of order *(außer Betrieb)*
out of place *(nicht am richtigen Platz)*
out of spite *(aus Bosheit)*
out of the ordinary *(ungewöhnlich)*
out of work *(arbeitslos)*

to some / a certain extent *(in gewissem Maße)*
to the point *(zur Sache)*

under oath *(unter Eid)*
under (no) obligation *([nicht] verpflichtet)*
under pressure *(unter Druck)*
under suspicion of *(unter Verdacht)*
under the impression that *(den Eindruck haben, dass)*
under the weather *(nicht ganz auf dem Posten)*
under way *(in der Mache)*

up to a point *(bis zu einem gewissen Grad)*
up to date *(auf dem neuesten Stand)*
up to no good *(nichts Gutes im Sinn)*
up to Jack / you / ... *(Jacks / Deine / Ihre / ... Sache)*

with regard / respect to *(mit Bezug auf)*
with the exception of *(mit Ausnahme von)*

without delay *(ohne Verzögerung)*
without (a) doubt *(ohne Zweifel)*
without exception *(ausnahmslos)*
without fail *(garantiert)*

Exercise 4 Complete the sentences with the correct preposition(s).

1 All the MPs voted __________ the exception __________ Mr Astley, who is ill.

2 Ben's doctor told him to go to hospital __________ delay.

3 Please don't leave out anything. I want an __________ depth report on the project.

4 The police found the murderer purely __________ chance.

5 Jody was wild as a teenager but __________ then __________ she settled down.

6 Obviously the media concentrates on things that are __________ the ordinary.

7 The unions rejected the offer __________ first sight but they didn't break off talks.

8 This was no accident; the machine was damaged __________ purpose.

9 Read the paper __________ leisure and let me know your opinion, okay?

10 Mrs Hadley supports the idea __________ a certain extent but she doesn't like the cost.

11 Some historians claim that the First World War was started __________ mistake.

12 __________ addition __________ accepting bribes, the managers speculated with the firm's money.

13 Unemployment is, __________ average, at its highest in northern England.

14 Why don't you do something useful __________ a change?

15 __________ the circumstances, it would be best if the minister resigned.

Exercise 5 Finish translating the sentences into English. Use prepositional expressions. You can consult a dictionary.

1 *Wir können uns bei meinen Eltern in London treffen.*

_______________________________________ in London.

2 *Becker war mit 17 Wimbledon-Sieger.*

____________ Wimbledon champion ____________ .

3 *Die Polizei tat nichts. Sie lachten nur über mich.*

The police did nothing. ____________________ .

4 *Der Journalist hat um ein Interview gebeten.*

The journalist ____________________________ .

5 *Du sollst Dich wegen Deines schlechten Benehmens entschuldigen.*

____________________________ your bad behaviour.

6 *Der Mann hat das Verbrechen gestanden.*

The man ______________________________ .

7 *Ich bestehe auf Ihre Anwesenheit bei der Sitzung.*

I ____________ your presence ______________ .

8 *Wir beziehen uns auf Ihren Brief vom 6. Juni.*

______________________________ of 6 June.

9 *Ich habe wenig Mitleid mit den verzogenen Kindern reicher Eltern.*

I ______________________________ the spoilt children ____________ .

10 *Die Gesellschaft hat eine Verpflichtung älteren Menschen gegenüber.*

_________________________________ older people.

11 *Ben erzählte uns ausführlich über seine Reise.*

Ben told us _________________________________ .

12 *In der Praxis sind solche Ideen völlig utopisch.*

______________________________ completely Utopian.

B 11 Fehler mit Phrasal Verbs

1 Grundwortschatz

① Sam never ~~stands up~~ before 10.
② I'll ~~wait on~~ you at the café, all right?

✓ ❶ Sam never **gets up** before 10.
✓ ❷ I'll **wait for** you at the café, all right?

→ Wie im Falle von festen Präposition-Verbindungen – siehe **B 10** – gehören auch **Phrasal Verbs** zu den häufigsten und gefährlichsten Fehlerquellen ❶, ❷.

→ **Phrasal Verbs** bestehen aus einem **Verb + einem Adverb**, z.B.:
break down *(eine Panne haben)*, **call in** *(vorbeischauen)*, **find out** *(herausfinden)*, **look into** *(untersuchen)*, **pick up** *(abholen)*, **stay up** *(aufbleiben)*

→ oder **einem Verb + einem Adverb + einer Präposition**, z.B.:
get along with *(mit jdm. auskommen)*, **get out of** *(aussteigen)*, **go out with** *(mit jdm. ausgehen)*, **look down on** *(herabsehen auf)*, **look forward to** *(sich freuen auf)*, **put up with** *(sich bieten lassen)*

→ Wie Sie sehen, ist es selten möglich, die Bedeutung eines **Phrasal Verbs** von den einzelnen Wörtern her zu erschließen. Deshalb ist es notwendig, alle Phrasal Verbs als eine Einheit auswendig zu lernen. Das folgende Verzeichnis stellt einige **gängige Phrasal Verbs** mit ihren deutschen Bedeutungen dar. Gibt es eine sinnvolle *non-phrasal* Alternative, ist diese in Klammern angegeben:

The car will **break down** if it has no oil. *(eine Panne haben)*
They had to **break off** (discontinue) the match. *(abbrechen)*
Why should women **bring up** (raise) children alone? *(erziehen)*
Henry Ford **built up** one of the biggest car firms in history. *(aufbauen)*
Why don't you **call in** (visit us) some time? *(vorbeischauen)*
Come to the board when I **call out** (say, shout) your name. *(ausrufen)*
Stop shouting. **Calm down** and we'll talk about it. *(sich beruhigen)*
We will **carry out** (perform) the operation tomorrow. *(durchführen)*
Harry, **clear up** (tidy) your room before you watch TV. *(aufräumen)*
I hope you'll **come back** (come again) soon. *(zurückkommen)*
Oh, hello, Mr Gregg. **Come in**, please. *(hereinkommen)*
Mary **fell down** / **over** and broke her arm. *(hin- / umfallen)*
You have to **fill in** / **out** (complete) a form to get a passport. *(ausfüllen)*
You can **find out** their number from the phone book. *(herausfinden)*
Two more prisoners **got away** (escaped) last night. *(entkommen)*
Don't **get in** / **on** (board) the train until it stops. *(einsteigen)*
We **got off** / **out of** the bus in the town centre. *(aussteigen)*

Get on (Continue) with your work while I am away. *(fortfahren)*
Does Jack always **get up** so early? *(aufstehen)*
She **gave away** a £10,000 when she won the lottery. *(verschenken)*
We must **give back** (return) the books. *(zurückgeben)*
When there's a fight our dog never **gives in** (surrenders). *(nachgeben)*
The doctor told him to **give up** (stop) smoking. *(aufgeben)*
When we **went back** (returned) our car had gone. *(zurückgehen)*
Well, **go on** (continue). What did she say then? *(weitermachen)*
Surely Ann doesn't want to **go out** with that awful man! *(ausgehen)*
I haven't lived here long. I **grew up** (was raised) in Norfolk. *(aufwachsen)*
I asked him to stop but he just **kept on** (continued). *(weitermachen)*
Don't do all the questions. **Leave out** (Omit) the last three. *(auslassen)*
Mary must **look after** (mind) her brother. *(sich kümmern um)*
Have you seen the dog? I've **looked for** him everywhere. *(suchen)*
I always **look forward to** Jill's parties. They're fun. *(sich freuen auf)*
Look out (Pay attention)! That car isn't going to stop. *(aufpassen)*
Look up (Find) the words in your dictionary. *(nachschlagen)*
Can you **make out** (recognize) what that sign says? *(erkennen)*
Please **pick up** (collect) the rubbish and take it away. *(aufheben)*
Please **put away** your books before going home. *(wegräumen)*
It's cold today. I'd **put on** (wear) a thicker pullover. *(anziehen)*
You can **put up** your tent over there. *(aufstellen)*
We must **set off** (leave) early tomorrow. *(aufbrechen)*
Can you **speak up** (speak louder)? I can't hear you. *(lauter sprechen)*
Don't forget to **stand up** (rise) when he comes in. *(aufstehen)*
Can I **stay up** and watch the late-night movie? *(aufbleiben)*
Did you **switch / turn** off the coffee-machine? *(ausschalten)*
Switch / turn on the television, please. *(an-/ einschalten)*
Take off (Remove) your coat and **sit down**. *(ausziehen, setzen)*
Jane's plane **takes off** (leaves) at three o'clock. *(starten)*
Always **try on** shoes before you buy them. *(anprobieren)*
For heaven's sake **turn down** the radio. We're talking. *(leiser stellen)*
Turn over the page for an explanation. *(umblättern)*
Turn up the radio, I want to listen to the news. *(lauter stellen)*
Keep quiet, please. You'll **wake up** (disturb) the baby. *(aufwecken)*
I was so tired that I didn't **wake up** for ten hours. *(aufwachen)*
Did you leave the plates for me to **wash up**? *(abwaschen, spülen)*
Can you **work out** (calculate) 2.7 + 0.3 x 6? *(ausrechnen)*
Please **write down** what I say. I won't say it again. *(aufschreiben)*

Exercise 1 Look at the German and complete the sentences with the correct form of the equivalent English phrasal verb.

1 ________________ when you cross the road. ↝ *aufpassen*

2 Can you ________________ how much tax I will have to pay? ↝ *ausrechnen*

3 A lot of young children ________________ to watch late night movies. ↝ *aufbeiben*

4 Nobody should be expected to ________________ everything they enjoy. ↝ *aufgeben*

5 American space probes ________________ from Cape Canaveral in Florida. ↝ *starten*

6 We can ________________ about hotels at the tourist information. ↝ herausfinden

7 I just can't ________________ what this letter really means. ↝ *erkennen*

8 Please ________________ the equipment before you leave. ↝ *wegräumen*

9 Helen ________________ ten pairs of shoes but she didn't buy any. ↝ *anprobieren*

10 Please ________________ the answer as soon as you know it. ↝ *ausrufen*

11 I ________________ at Mary's on my way to work tomorrow if you like. ↝ *vorbeischauen*

12 Don't forget to ________________ the post on your way home. ↝ *abholen*

13 The fans ________________________________ the new football season. ↝ *sich freuen auf*

14 Charles Dickens ________________ in very difficult circumstances. ↝ *aufwachsen*

2 Aufbauwortschatz

→ Hier sind weitere **Phrasal Verbs** aus dem Aufbauwortschatz.

Don't touch that bomb. It might **blow up** (explode). *(explodieren)*
Some terrorists **blew up** a jet over Lockerby. *(sprengen)*
He had no money so he **broke into** (robbed) a bank. *(einbrechen)*
Four men **broke out** of the prison last night. *(ausbrechen)*
Tom is ill because he **breathed in** (inhaled) some gas. *(einatmen)*
I want to listen to your chest. **Breathe out** slowly, please. *(ausatmen)*
We'll have to **call off** (cancel) the match. *(absagen)*
We must **check in** an hour before the flight. *(sich abfertigen lassen)*
Please return your key when you **check out** (leave). *(abreisen)*
He was sad but he **cheered up** when she phoned. *(aufheitern)*
We **cleared up** (solved) the problem by talking about it. *(lösen)*
We are **doing up** (decorating) our house. *(renovieren)*
I always **drop off** (go to sleep) during TV programmes. *(einnicken)*
Taking the wrong road, we **ended up** (landed) in Bath. *(enden, landen)*
They are always fighting. When did they **fall out**? *(sich zerstreiten)*
Don't forget to **fill up** the car, will you? *(tanken)*
Let's **fix up** (arrange) a meeting in July, shall we? *(arrangieren)*
Do Sally and Jill **get along / on with** each other? *(sich vertragen)*
Is Ann **getting on** (progressing) with her work? *(vorankommen)*
We try and **go away** (take a break) at least twice a year. *(verreisen)*
Our boss always **goes off** (leaves) early on a Friday. *(fortgehen)*
Don't walk so fast. I can't **keep up**. *(Schritt halten)*
They are planning to **knock down** (demolish) that church. *(abreißen)*
Wait, don't **hang up** (replace the receiver). *(Hörer auflegen)*
Ian? **Hang on** (Wait a moment). I'll get him. *(am Apparat bleiben)*
The firm is **laying off** (dismissing) more men next month. *(entlassen)*
Don't trust her. She's **let down** (abandoned) everybody. *(im Stich lassen)*
You can borrow my car if you **look after** it. *(auf etwas aufpassen)*
I wonder who **made up** (thought of) these stories. *(ausdenken)*
Don't take a bus. I'll **pick** you **up** (collect) at the airport. *(abholen)*
He **pointed out** (indicated) that it was late. *(hinweisen auf)*
One moment. I'll **put** you **through** to Mr Gregg now. *(durchstellen)*
That shop has **put up** (increased) its prices by 10%. *(erhöhen)*
Don't go to a hotel. We can **put** you **up** (accommodate). *(unterbringen)*
I won't **put up with** (tolerate) that behaviour. *(sich abfinden mit)*
Would you like to **see over / round** (view) our new flat? *(besichtigen)*
Ian didn't like Bath at first but he's **settled in** now. *(sich einleben)*
Stop **showing off** (boasting). You're no genius, either. *(angeben)*
He was dead when the doctor **showed up** (arrived). *(auftauchen)*
He **started off** (began) by telling us the history of the play. *(beginnen)*
The firm is **taking on** (hiring) some more workers. *(einstellen)*
Don't **tear up** (destroy) that letter. I haven't read it yet. *(zerreißen)*
The play **turned out** to be very good. *(sich herausstellen)*
Turn over, please. I want to look at your back. *(sich umdrehen)*

We had already begun when Al **turned up** (arrived). *(aufkreuzen)*
I'm not going to **wait on** (serve) you. Get your food yourself. *(bedienen)*
I'll be late tonight. Don't **wait up for** me. *(aufbleiben wegen)*
My headache **wore off** (got slowly better) during the day. *(nachlassen)*
I can't **work** you **out** (understand), Sue. You should be happy. *(verstehen)*
The old brakes have **worn out**. *(aufgebraucht sein)*

Exercise 2

Complete the phrasal verbs with the correct particle.

after, around, in, off (2), on (3), out (5), up (5)

1 Have you got the space to put ______ some friends of mine next weekend?

2 Modern phones play music to you while you're hanging ______ .

3 Rubber is cheap but it wears ______ quite quickly.

4 I wish people wouldn't keep telling me to cheer ______ .

5 Bureaucrats make ______ some rules for purely egotistical reasons.

6 They threw ______ the governor because so many prisoners broke _____ .

7 Dick and Jane don't get ______ very well. They're always falling ______ with each other.

8 We arrive at the hotel at 3 and then we've got an hour to settle ______ .

9 They had to call ______ the match because of all the violence.

10 We could get more for our flat if we did it ______ a bit. It looks awful.

11 The girl who waited ____ our table looked _________ us very well.

12 I dropped ______ in the bus and missed my stop.

13 My boss loves pointing ______ other people's mistakes.

14 I turned ______ on time but I still had to hang ___________ for an hour.

Exercise 3 Replace the verbs with a phrasal of similar meaning from the list.

1 It is a crime to **hire** › ________________ illegal immigrants.

2 We are **performing** › ________________ the tests next week.

3 You shouldn't **remove** › ________________ your clothes on Arabian beaches.

4 The company is **investigating** › ________________ the matter at the moment.

5 After her divorce Clare, **destroyed** › ________________ all her photos of Tom.

6 All library books must be **returned** › ________________ within 14 days.

7 Were you able to **arrange** › ________________ an interview with the Beckers?

8 Terry loves to **boast** › ________________ in front of pretty women.

9 All visitors have to **wear** › ________________ a hard hat when they go down the mine.

10 The police still haven't **solved** › ________________ the crime.

11 Unfortunately, you **omitted** › ________________ some important points.

12 We plan to **leave** › ________________ very early because of the hot weather.

13 Nobody should have to **tolerate** › ________________ that kind of behaviour.

14 Fingers Fred **escaped** › ________________ as he was being taken to court.

15 The church tower was **demolished** › ________________ by a hot air balloon.

16 Everybody **rose** › ________________ when the judge entered the room.

carrying out, cleared up, fix up, given back, got away, knocked down, left out, looking into, put on, put up with, set off, show off, stood up, take off, take on, tore up

B 12 Wort- und Ausdrucksfehler

1 Falsche Freunde

→ Sehr viele Wörter sind im Deutschen und im Englischen ähnlich. Da die Bedeutung dieser Wörter in den beiden Sprachen oft ebenfalls dieselbe ist, können wir die Bedeutung solcher Wörter leicht erschließen.

→ Es gibt jedoch eine kleine Gruppe von Wörtern, die wir **False Friends** nennen, weil die Bedeutung von ähnlich aussehenden Wörtern abweicht. Nehmen wir als Beispiel das deutsche Wort „miserabel“:
Hört oder liest man das englische Wort **miserable**, meint man fast automatisch, dass dieses Wort – wie das deutsche – auch etwa „erbärmlich“ heißen muss. Dies ist aber nicht der Fall. Das deutsche Wort „miserabel“ lautet auf Englisch **awful** oder **useless**, während das englische Wort **miserable** in Deutsch „deprimiert“ oder „niedergeschlagen“ bedeutet. Die beiden Wörter sind also **False Friends**.

→ Leider gibt es andere „Freunde“, die mal „treu“ und mal „falsch“ sind. Solche Freunde hat man natürlich besonders gerne.
Ein einfaches Beispiel ist das deutsche Verb „machen“:
Dieses Wort ähnelt sehr dem englischen Wort **make**, und in vielen Anwendungen – zum Beispiel **make a bed**, **make a noise** oder **make a table** – ist dies von der Bedeutung her auch der Fall. Bedeutet aber „machen“ etwa „erledigen“ oder „durchführen“, dann verwenden wir im Englischen nicht **make**, sondern **do**, wie zum Bespiel in den Ausdrücken **do homework**, **do the garden** oder **do the shopping**.

→ In den folgenden Listen finden Sie die geläufigsten **False Friends**. Links steht das deutsche Wort. In der Mitte finden Sie einen Satz mit der richtigen Anwendung des entsprechenden englischen Wortes. Rechts ist der typische Fehler angegeben.

→ **Verben:**

aufstehen	Tom always **gets up** very early.	~~stands up~~
bemerken	**Did you notice** anything unusual?	~~Did you remark~~
bringen	Can you **take** me to school, Mum?	~~bring~~
fahren	Ann **goes** to work by bus.	~~drives~~
irritieren	**Don't distract** me when I'm working.	~~Don't irritate~~
meinen	Sarah **thinks** Jane will get the job.	~~means~~
machen	**Have you done** your homework yet?	~~Have you made~~
spenden	Wendy often **donates** money to charity.	~~spends~~
starten	Jane's plane **takes off** at 4.45.	~~starts~~
übersehen	I **overlooked** three mistakes.	~~oversaw~~

→ **Substantive**:

Chips	Two packets of **crisps**, please.	~~chips~~
Frau	Is Ann your brother's **wife**?	~~woman~~
Fremde	You shouldn't go out with **strangers**.	~~foreigners~~
Land	Saxony is a German [federal] **state**.	~~land~~
Mann	Her **husband** has got his own firm.	~~man~~
Menü	I'll have the **set meal**, please.	~~menu~~
Pause	We **had a break** at 3.	~~made a pause~~
Pension	We stayed in a cheap **guest house**.	~~pension~~
Politik	What's the government's **roads policy**?	~~roads politic(s)~~
Preis	Ellen won a **prize** of £100.	~~price~~
Rente	Mrs Bond lives off a small **pension**.	~~rent~~
Rezept	Here's a **prescription for** painkillers.	~~recipe for~~
See	There are a lot of **lakes** in the Eifel.	~~seas~~

→ **Adjektive, Adverbien**:

aktuell	This isn't the **current** problem.	~~actual~~
brav	Tom's a **good** / **well-behaved** boy.	~~brave~~
dezent	Please wear **discreet** / **subdued** clothes.	~~decent~~
desinteressiert	Bob's **uninterested** in school.	~~disinterested~~
dick	Their dog is much too **fat**.	~~thick~~
eventuell	**Maybe** I'll come to the party.	~~eventually~~
komfortabel	They own a **luxurious** flat in Paris.	~~comfortable~~
nächste	This is the **nearest** bus stop to our flat.	~~next~~
neueste	Have you heard the **latest** news?	~~newest~~
plump	Brenda's a very **awkward** / **clumsy** girl.	~~plump~~
sensibel	Ben's very **sensitive** about his job.	~~sensible~~
seriös	Carr & Co is a very **reputable** firm.	~~serious~~
sympathisch	Sarah is a very **nice** / **likeable** girl.	~~sympathetic~~

Exercise 1 Finish translating the sentences into English.

1 *Mach dir keine Sorgen. Der Hund ist meistens brav.*

_________________ . The dog is usually _________________ .

2 *Ich habe wenig Zeit. Kannst du das Treppenhaus machen?*

I haven't much time. _____________________ the stairs?

3 *In islamischen Ländern sollten Sie sich dezent kleiden.*

In Islamic ___________ you should ______________________ .

4 *Seine Rente reicht nicht mal aus, die Miete zu zahlen.*

His pension isn't even sufficient ___________________________ .

5 *Heute muss ich die Kinder in die Schule bringen.*

I ____________________________________ to school today.

6 *Eine Ernährung auf der Basis von Chips und Keksen ist kaum gesund.*

A diet of ______________________________ is hardly healthy.

7 *Leider sind viele sogenannte „Finanzberater“ nicht seriös.*

Unfortunately, a lot of so-called “financial consultants” __________

______________________ .

8 *Viele Restaurants bieten ein preiswertes Touristenmenü an.*

A lot of restaurants offer ______________________________ .

9 *Mit Fremden scheint Markus zunächst unfreundlich zu sein.*

At first Markus seems ______________________________ .

10 *Wie viele Länder gibt es in der Bundesrepublik?*

______________________________ in the federal republic?

11 *Rezepte sind für Patienten nicht mehr völlig kostenlos.*

_____________________ are no longer completely free

_____________________ .

12 *Ich finde, dass Jane eine sehr sympathische Frau geworden ist.*

I think that Jane has become ___________________________ .

13 *Die Deutschen spenden mehr Geld als andere Europäer.*

The Germans ______________________________________

other Europeans.

14 *Begabte Menschen sind eben auch oft sensible Menschen.*

It's a fact that ____________________________ are also often

_____________________________ .

15 *Wir möchten uns eine schöne Pension kaufen.*

We want to buy ________________________________ .

16 *Kann ich bitte die aktuellste Ausgabe des Fahrplans haben?*

Can I please have _____________________________ edition

________________ .

2 Wörter, die leicht verwechselt werden

→ Bei **False Friends** handelt es sich um die unterschiedliche Bedeutung von Wörtern, die im Deutschen und Englischen ähnlich aussehen. Bei **Confusibles** dagegen handelt es sich um englische Wortpaare, die leicht verwechselt werden können. (Auch Muttersprachler haben mit ihnen Probleme.)

Grundwortschatz

→ **Verben**:

become	Wendy wants to **become** a nurse. *(werden)*
get	Can I **get** stamps here? *(bekommen)*

borrow	We **borrowed** a lot of money to buy our flat. *(sich etwas leihen)*
lend	Never **lend** Joe money. He never pays it back. *(jdm. etwas leihen)*

Diese beiden Verben sind – wie **come** / **go** – **richtungsbedingt**. Wenn die Richtung zum Sprecher hin geht, benutzen wir **borrow**. Wenn die Richtung andersherum läuft, dann benutzen wir **lend**.

lay	The teacher **laid** the tests on the desk. *(legen)*
lie	Why don't you **lie** down for an hour? *(liegen)*
lie	Don't **lie** – I saw you do it with my own eyes. *(lügen)*

Das Verb **lay** hat immer ein Objekt und ist unregelmäßig – **lay**, **laid**, **laid**. Das Verb **lie** hat zwei Bedeutungen. Im Sinne von „liegen" ist es unregelmäßig – **lie**, **lay**, **lain** – und in der Bedeutung „lügen" regelmäßig – **lie**, **lied**, **lied**. Gleich welcher Bedeutung hat **lie** kein Objekt.

take place	The meeting will **take place** at 3 on Friday. *(stattfinden)*
happen / occur	The accident **happened** / **occurred** in fog. *(passieren)*

Am besten benutzt man **take place** nur in Verbindung mit planmäßigen Handlungen. Zufällige oder plötzliche Ereignisse sind besser mit **happen** bzw. **occur** ausgedrückt.

→ **Substantive**:

play	Hamlet is a **play** by Shakespeare. *(Theaterstück)*
game	Let's have a **game** of cards tonight. *(Spiel)*

recipe	Mrs Patel gave me a **recipe** for curry. *(Rezept)*
prescription	You can only get this medicine on **prescription**. *(Rezept)*
receipt	Don't forget to ask for a **receipt** for your meal. *(Quittung)*

variety	The moon has no **variety**. It is just a rock. *(Vielseitigkeit)*
versatility	He has no **versatility**. He acts only comic roles. *(Vielseitigkeit)*

Die Wörter **variety** (Adj.: **various**) und **versatility** (Adj.: **versatile**) sind gleichbedeutend, werden aber unterschiedlich eingesetzt. Wir können

variety nur im Zusammenhang mit Sachen benutzen, **versatile** dagegen ausschließlich mit Menschen und Tieren. Wir können also nicht sagen: *The Dutch province of Flevoland is an area of great ~~versatility~~.*

town Southport is a seaside **town** near Liverpool. *(Stadt)*
city / town Norwich is a beautiful **city / town** in Norfolk. *([Dom-]Stadt)*
Im Englischen benutzen wir **city** nur im Sinne von „Domstadt" – z.B. *York, Norwich, Durham* – und für einige wichtige Großstädte wie *Bradford, Leeds* und *Newcastle*. Das Wort **town** können wir dagegen immer verwenden. Der deutsche Gebrauch von „City" in den Bedeutungen „Stadtmitte", „Altstadt" und gar „Einkaufszentrum" ist im Englischen nicht möglich.

→ **Adjektive, Adverbien**:
big It's hard to park **big** cars nowadays. *(groß [geräumig])*
great Bach was a **great** composer. *(groß [großartig])*
Das Wort **big** – oder **large** – heißt „physisch groß". Das Adjektiv **great** dagegen bedeutet „geistig groß" oder „großartig".

finished Have you **finished** the letters, Sally? *(fertig [„erledigt"])*
ready Jill is never **ready** when I call for her. *(fertig [„bereit"])*
Wenn wir ausdrücken möchten, dass eine Tätigkeit zu Ende gegangen ist, dann benutzen wir **finish**. Handelt es sich um „fertig" im Sinne von „bereit sein", dann gebrauchen wir **ready**.

happy We're very **happy** in our new house. *(glücklich)*
lucky Jill was **lucky** to get such a good job. *(Glück haben)*
Das Wort **happy** kann immer durch **satisfied** („zufrieden") ersetzt werden. Wenn dies nicht der Fall ist, dann sollten Sie **lucky** benutzen.

heavy Please help me carry this **heavy** case. *(schwer)*
difficult I can't answer these **difficult** questions. *(schwer [schwierig])*
Heavy kann durch **big** ersetzt werden und **difficult** durch **hard**.

industrial Manchester is an **industrial** city in England. *(industriell)*
industrious Bob isn't a very **industrious** pupil. *(fleißig, emsig)*

little They've got a lovely **little** puppy. *(klein [niedlich])*
small **Small** cars are easier to park than big ones. *(klein)*
Wenn wir über physische Größe reden wollen, benutzen wir **small**, außer wenn wir gleichzeitig „niedlich" meinen. Dann verwenden wir **little**.

practical Children like doing **practical** things at school. *(praktisch)*
practicable It's a nice idea, but it's just not **practicable**. *(durchführbar)*
Wir benutzen **practical** für praktische Tätigkeiten. Ist die Tätigkeit nur schwer durchführbar, verwenden wir **practicable**. Beachten Sie, dass **practicable** häufig in Verneinungen und Fragen vorkommt:
Do you really think that's **practicable**?

tasty These tuna sandwiches are **tasty**. *(lecker)*
tasteful(ly) Their house is very **tastefully** furnished. *(geschmackvoll)*

→ **Verschiedenes**:
advice He took no notice of the doctor's **advice**. *(Rat[schlag])*
advise I **advise** you to stop smoking, Mrs Benn. *(beraten)*
practice Jenny is much better in theory than in **practice**. *(Praxis)*
practise Concert pianists **practise** several hours a day. *(üben)*
In beiden Fällen endet das Substantiv auf **-ice**, das Verb auf **-ise**.

loose Don't shake the bottle. The cap is **loose**. *(locker)*
lose Did Ann **lose** her ticket again? *(verlieren)*
Das Adjektiv **loose** bedeutet locker („nicht fest") bzw. nicht zusammen gebunden („lose").

principal His **principal** argument was the high cost. *(Haupt-)*
principle It's a matter of **principle**. *(Prinzip)*

stationary My car was **stationary** when he ran into me. *(stehend)*
stationery We spend too much on **stationery** in our office. *(Schreibwaren)*

Exercise 2 Complete the sentences with the correct words. You must use both words, sometimes more than once.

1 A little ____________ often is better than ________________ for hours now and then. *practice, practising*

2 You will _______ your button if you're not careful. It is ________. *loose, lose*

3 Sally was _________ to win the lottery. I bet she's ___________ now. *happy, lucky*

4 The work __________________ was the ____________ that generated the industrial revolution. Some historians see it as the ____________ cause of this development. *principal, principle*

5 You will never _______ a good job unless you ________ qualifications. If you're not careful, you'll ____________ "professionally unemployed". *become, get*

6 Are you ___________ to leave now? I've ______________ loading the car. *finished, ready*

7 It's quite simple. All ______ are ________ , but not all ________ are ________ . ~ *cities, towns*

8 "Can you ________ me my bus fare?" "Sorry. I had to ________ my fare myself today." ~ *borrow, lend*

9 Do you think it is ______________ for Tom to look for a ____________ job like a mechanic? He can't even switch on the TV without help. ~ *practical, practicable*

10 Ben had to ________ down after ____________ the floor tiles. It was hard work. ~ *laying, lie*

11 The idea that Africans aren't __________ enough to develop an __________ society is complete nonsense.
~ *industrial, industrious*

12 Don't forget to get a __________ for the things we need for the __________ . It's a business meal. ~ *receipt, recipe*

13 You must introduce more ____________ into your lessons, Miss Brown. Your lack of ____________ is your big weakness.
~ *variety, versatility*

14 I don't want to watch the football ____________ . Why don't we go and watch the new ____________ at the fringe theatre tonight? ~ *game, play*

15 It was really ______________ to move the ____________ wardrobe down the stairs. We needed a __________ van to transport it to the new flat.
~ *big, difficult, heavy*

16 The concert ________________ in the park behind the castle. Suddenly, a funny incident ______________ , when a dog started howling during the final violin solo.
~ *occur, take place*

17 It's always the same – he never takes any ____________ . When I tried to ____________ him on how to spend his money he just laughed at me. ~ *advice, advise*

Aufbauwortschatz

→ **Verben**:

abuse Some parents **abuse** their children. *(missbrauchen)*
misuse If you **misuse** the machine, it will break. *(falsch bedienen)*
Diese Verben werden sehr häufig verwechselt. Das Verb **abuse** hat die Bedeutung „moralisch schlecht behandeln". Das Wort **misuse** dagegen ist moralisch neutral. Es heißt einfach „fehlerhaft bedienen".

affect Smoking **affects** your health. *(beeinflussen)*
effect He **effected** his escape by taking a hostage. *(bewirken)*
Die unterschiedliche Bedeutung von **affect** und **effect** wird häufig übersehen. Statt **affect** können Sie **have an effect on** gebrauchen und statt **effect** kann man **carry out successfully** benutzen.

arbitrate They had to ask a court to **arbitrate**. *(schlichten)*
mediate The EU is trying to **mediate** in Bosnia. *(vermitteln)*
Bei **arbitrate** handelt es sich um den Versuch, unterschiedliche Positionen neutral auszuwerten, um ein Urteil zu bilden. Bei **mediate** versucht dagegen der Vermittler, die Parteien durch Überreden zu einigen.

avoid I tried to **avoid** paying too much tax. *(vermeiden)*
evade **Evading** responsibilities is dishonest. *(ausweichen)*
Avoid hat keine moralische Implikation. Es bedeutet, einer ungünstigen Situation auszuweichen. **Evade** dagegen meint einen illegalen bzw. unmoralischen Versuch, rechtmäßigen Verpflichtungen zu entkommen.

convince He tried to **convince** me of his views. *(überzeugen)*
persuade Can't I **persuade** you to forget the plan? *(überreden)*
Benutzen Sie **convince** für theoretische bzw. abstrakte Sachen und **persuade** für praktische Tätigkeiten oder Vorgänge: **convince s.b. to believe** / **think s.th.**, **persuade s.b. to do s.th.**

imply Are you **implying** that I'm wrong? *(unterstellen)*
infer From his attitude we **inferred** he didn't like us. *(erschließen)*
Diese Verben werden häufig verwechselt. Das Wort **imply** heißt **suggest** im Sinne von „andeuten". **Infer** dagegen bedeutet, „ein Urteil bilden".

prescribe FIFA **prescribes** the rules of football. *(vorschreiben)*
proscribe The EU **proscribed** the export of animals. *(verbieten)*

repel The idea of eating dogs **repels** most Europeans. *(abstoßen)*
repulse The soldiers **repulsed** the attack on the town. *(abwehren)*
Diese Wörter werden verwechselt wegen des Adjektivs **repulsive**, also „abstoßend". Als Verben jedoch haben sie völlig unterschiedliche Bedeutungen.

→ **Adjektive, Adverbien:**

biannual We bring out a **biannual** report, in March and October. *(halbjährlich)*

biennial The fair is **biennial**. It takes place every other May. *(zweijährlich)*

Der häufigste Fehler ist hier, **biannual** statt **biennial** zu gebrauchen. Das Problem ist jedoch leicht zu umgehen. Für **biannual** benutzen Sie **twice a year** und für **biennial** verwenden Sie **every other year**.

continual I just can't accept these **continual** lies. *(ständig)*

continuous We came back early because of the **continuous** rain. *(unaufhörlich)*

Viele Schüler/innen verwenden **continual**, wenn sie **continuous** meinen, wie zum Beispiel in dem Satz:
I can't stand this continual (**continuous**) noise.
Merken Sie sich, dass **continual** „immer wieder mit Unterbrechungen" bedeutet. Das Wort **continuous** bedeutet dagegen „fortlaufend und ununterbrochen".

definite Can you let us have a **definite** offer by Friday? *(eindeutig)*

definitive This is our **definitive** offer. Take it or leave it. *(endgültig)*

Das Wort **definite** kann man durch **precise** bzw. **exact** ersetzen; es ist das Gegenteil von **approximate**, **rough**. Bei **definitive** handelt es sich dagegen um etwas, das nicht zur Diskussion steht, also „das letzte Wort".

economic Russia's **economic** problems are immense. *(ökonomisch)*

economical Are diesel cars more **economical** than petrol ones? *(wirtschaftlich)*

Bei diesem Wortpaar ist der häufigste Fehler, **economical** statt **economic** zu verwenden, wie zum Beispiel in dem Satz:
The USA won't give economical (**economic**) aid to dictatorships.
Diese Verwechslung ist leicht zu umgehen, indem Sie an das deutsche Wort „ökonomisch" denken.

sociable Jill is a friendly, **sociable** sort of girl. *(gesellig)*

social Britain has many **social** problems. *(Sozial-)*

Es kann passieren, dass Sie gelegentlich **social** statt **sociable** sehen.
Jill is a social (**sociable**) sort of girl.
Dies ist jedoch ein eindeutiger Fehler.

Das deutsche Wort „sozial" im Sinne von „sozialdenkend" kann im Englischen nur durch **socially-conscious** ausgedrückt werden.

Verschiedenes:

licence May I see your fishing **licence**, please? *(Berechtigungsschein)*

license I'm not **licensed** to drive yet. *(Erlaubnis haben)*

Merken Sie sich, dass das Substantiv mit **-ce** und das Verb mit **-se** geschrieben werden. Das Verb wird oft im Passiv gebraucht.

Exercise 3 Tick (✔) the correct alternative.

1 Some people don't realize it is a criminal offence to ↝ avoid ( ) evade ( ) ↝ taxation.

2 What right have you to ↝ prescribe ( ) proscribe ( ) ↝ how I live my life?

3 There are ↝ biannual ( ) biennial ( ) ↝ exams in the summer and at Christmas.

4 Cars are more ↝ economic ( ) economical ( ) ↝ nowadays.

5 What's wrong with you? You aren't very ↝ sociable ( ) social ( ) ↝ today.

6 We haven't got a ↝ licence ( ) license ( ) ↝ to sell alcohol after 11 pm.

7 Child pornography ↝ repels ( ) repulses ( ) ↝ all decent people.

8 Are you ↝ inferring ( ) implying ( ) ↝ that you don't agree with the decision?

9 Asia Briggs wrote the ↝ definite ( ) definitive ( ) ↝ work on Victorian England.

Exercise 4 Underline the mistakes and correct them. There is one mistake in each sentence.

1 Bremen is the smallest German land.

2 The injured dog was laying at the side of the road.

3 Don't drive for two hours. This drug can effect your eyesight.

4 The festival happens every August.

5 You can't make a pause until you have finished the job.

6 You needn't wear black but please wear decent colours.

7 Eventually we can get a map at that garage over there.

8 It's easy to hurt Ann's feelings. She's too sensible for this world.

9 The wife in front of me just could not decide what she wanted.

10 Did you remark that policeman?

11 My teacher adviced me to go on a holiday course in England.

12 Can you borrow me your dictionary, please?

B 13 Häufige Rechtschreibprobleme

1 Die Nachsilben *-able* / *-ible*

① I once saw a film about an ~~invisable~~ man.
② Sarah is a very ~~likable~~ girl.
③ Is this machine ~~moveable~~?

✓ ❶ I once saw a film about an **invisible** man.
✓ ❷ Sarah is a very **likeable** girl.
✓ ❸ Is this machine **movable**?

→ Die Nachsilben -**able** und -**ible** haben dieselbe Bedeutung, nämlich „zu etwas imstande sein“. Sie entsprechen also deutsche Nachsilben wie *-bar* und *-lich*.
In der Schule gibt es zwei Fehlerquellen bei diesen Nachsilben. Die erste Fehlerquelle ist die Verwechslung von -**able** und -**ible** ❶.
Die meisten gängigen Wörter dieser Gruppe – zum Beispiel **acceptable**, **believable** *(glaubwürdig)*, **comfortable**, **eatable** *(genießbar)*, enden auf **-able**. Im Zweifelsfall ist es also ratsam **-able** zu wählen.

Wörter, die auf -**ible** enden, kommen verhältnismäßig selten vor. Merken Sie sich jedoch die folgenden Beispiele:

accessible *(erreichbar, zugänglich)*; **audible** *(hörbar)*; **comprehensible** *(verständlich)*; **contemptible** *(verachtenswert)*; **edible** *(essbar)*; **legible** *(lesbar)*; **irresistible** *(unwiderstehlich)*; **permissible** *(zulässig)*; **plausible** *(glaubwürdig)*; **possible** *(möglich)*; **responsible** *(verantwortlich, verantwortungsvoll)*; **sensible** *(vernünftig)*; **visible** *(sichtbar)*

→ Der zweite Fehler hat mit dem Wegfall des stummen -**e** zu tun ❷, ❸.
Die Grundregel lautet, dass ein stummes -**e** entfällt: **advise** / **advisable** *(ratsam)*; **believe** / **believable** *(glaubhaft)*; **reproduce** / **reproducible** *(reproduzierbar)*.

Ausnahmen – wegen des **weichen g**- bzw. **c-Lautes** – bilden:
changeable *(wechselhaft)*; **manageable** *(fügsam, handlich)*; **noticeable** *(merkbar)*; **peaceable** *(friedfertig)*; **pronounceable** *(aussprechbar)*

Andere Ausnahmen, die man sich einfach merken muss, sind:
likeable *(sympathisch)*; **sizeable** *(ziemlich groß, beachtlich)*

Exercise 1 Put in the correct English equivalent of the German words.

1 It is not ________________ for people under 18 to buy alcohol. ↝ *zulässig*

2 Are you sure these mushrooms are ________________ ? ↝ *essbar*

3 Don't worry. The scratch on my car is hardly ________________ . ↝ *merkbar*

4 Jane is a very ________________ girl. ↝ *sympathisch*

5 I don't think that is a ________________ suggestion. ↝ *vernünftig*

6 There's been so much rain that the pitch is ________________ . ↝ *unspielbar*

7 Would a payment of £500 be ________________ to you? ↝ *akzeptabel*

8 The mountains weren't ________________ because of low cloud. ↝ *sichtbar*

9 We'll have to take out a ________________ loan if we go on holiday. ↝ *beachtlich*

10 We need a ________________ person to babysit for us tonight. ↝ *verantwortungsvoll*

11 I'm told the Russians are very friendly, ________________ people. ↝ *gastfreundlich*

12 It's not ________________ to sunbathe for too long. ↝ *ratsam*

13 You can't say "hearable". You have to say "________________". ↝ *hörbar*

14 You must fill in the form in clear, ________________ handwriting. ↝ *lesbar*

15 Welsh place names look totally ________________ . ↝ *unaussprechbar*

16 Some of the pages are not ________________ with a photocopier. ↝ *reproduzierbar*

2 Die Nachsilben *-ise* / *-ize*

① I hate the ~~advertizing~~ on TV.
② She didn't ~~recognise~~ me at first.

✓ ❶ I hate the **advertising** on TV.
✓ ❷ She didn't **recognize** me at first.

→ In der Vergangenheit gab es eine klare Konvention über die Anwendung von -**ize** und -**ise**.
Die -**ize**-Endung – zum Beispiel **characterize** *(charakterisieren);* **economize** *(sparen);* **industrialize**; **organize**; **recognize** *(erkennen)*; **realize** *(bemerken)* – wurde bevorzugt.

→ Die -**ise**-Endung dagegen fanden wir bei folgenden Verben:
advertise *(werben, inserieren);* **advise** *(beraten);* **compromise** *(einen Kompromiss schließen);* **despise** *(verachten);* **disguise** *(verkleiden, verstellen, tarnen);* **practise** *(üben, ausüben);* **promise** *(versprechen);* **revise** *(wiederholen);* **supervise** *(beaufsichtigen);* **surprise** *(überraschen);* **televise** *(im Fernsehen übertragen, senden)*

Vor allem im britischen Englisch (BE) wird die -**ise**-Endung immer beliebter und mindestens eine namhafte Zeitschrift – *The Economist* – benutzt ausschließlich diese Endung. Im amerikanischen Englisch (AE) dagegen wird die -**ize**-Endung weiterhin verwendet.

Exercise 2 Think of the new **British** convention about -**ise** / -**ize**. Underline those verbs in the list that can take the suffix -**ize**. There are 11 of them.

1	advertise	12	industrialise
2	advise	13	legalise
3	civilise	14	organise
4	colonise	15	promise
5	compromise	16	practise
6	criticise	17	realise
7	despise	18	recognise
8	disguise	19	revise
9	economise	20	standardise
10	emphasise	21	surprise
11	exercise	22	televise

3 Wörter, die oft falsch geschrieben werden

① We were all ~~embarassed~~ when he got drunk.
② Tom is getting very ~~independant~~ as he gets older.
③ Don't ~~exagerate~~. I only had four beers.

✓ ❶ We were all **embarrassed** when he got drunk.
✓ ❷ Tom is getting very **independent** as he gets older.
✓ ❸ Don't **exaggerate**. I only had four beers.

→ Die folgenden Wörter werden – auch von Muttersprachlern – oft falsch geschrieben. Die fettgedruckten Buchstaben in der linken Spalte sind besonders zu beachten. Die rechte Spalte zeigt die am häufigsten vorkommenden Fehler.

→ **Verben**, **Verbformen**:

a**cc**o**mm**odate	*unterbringen*	~~accomodate~~
assa**ss**inated	*ermordet*	~~assasinated~~
ben**e**fit, ben**e**fi**t**ed	*von etwas profitieren*	~~benifit, benifitted~~
bu**s**ed, bu**s**ing (AE)	*mit dem Bus befördern*	~~bussed, bussing~~
co**mm**e**m**orate	*gedenken*	~~comem(m)orate~~
e**m**ba**rr**a**ss**	*in Verlegenheit bringen*	~~embar(r)as(s)~~
exa**gg**erate	*übertreiben*	~~exagerate~~
for**e**cas**t**	*vorhersagen*	~~forcast(e)~~
for**e**warn	*vorwarnen*	~~forwarn~~
fu**l**fi**l**	*erfüllen*	~~fullfill~~
ha**r**a**ss**	*schikanieren*	~~harras(s)~~
re**c**o**mm**end	*empfehlen*	~~reccomend~~
sw**a**p	*austauschen*	~~swop~~

→ **Substantive**:

a**cc**o**mm**odation	*Unterkunft*	~~acom(m)odation~~
a**cq**uaint**a**nce	*Bekannte(r)*	~~aquaintence~~
ad**d**ress	*Adresse*	~~adress~~
defend**a**nt	*Angeklagte(r)*	~~defendent~~
depend**a**nt	*Abhängige(r)*	~~dependent~~
dialog**ue**	*Dialog*	~~dialog~~
dis**k**	*Computerdiskette*	~~disc~~
e**m**ba**rr**a**ss**ment	*Verlegenheit*	~~embar(r)as(s)ment~~
encyclo**pe**dia	*Enzyklopädie*	~~encyclopaedie~~
exa**gg**eration	*Übertreibung*	~~exageration~~
fu**l**fi**l**ment	*Erfüllung*	~~ful(l)fil(l)ment~~
gover**n**ment	*Regierung*	~~goverment~~
ha**r**a**ss**ment	*Schikane*	~~harras(s)ment~~
independ**e**nce	*Unabhängigkeit*	~~independance~~
insta**l**ment	*Rate, Fortsetzung*	~~installment~~

jewe**ll**ery	*Schmuck*	~~jewel(e)ry~~
ma**rri**age	*Ehe*	~~mar(r)ige~~
naiv**e**ty	*Naivität*	~~naivity~~
parl**ia**ment	*Parlament*	~~parlament~~
progra**m**	*Computerprogramm*	~~programm~~
progra**mme**	*Programm, Sendung*	~~programm~~
represent**a**tive	*Vertreter*	~~represente(i)tive~~
stor**ey**	*Stockwerk*	~~story~~

→ **Adjektive, Adverbien**:

advis**o**ry	*beratend*	~~advisery~~
bi**as**ed	*voreingenommen*	~~bies(s)ed~~
con**sc**ient**i**ous	*gewissenhaft*	~~cons(ch)ientous~~
conv**e**ni**e**nt	*günstig, praktisch*	~~conviniant~~
depend**e**nt	*abhängig*	~~dependant~~
eig**hth**	*achte*	~~eig(h)tth~~
e**m**ba**rr**a**ss**ed	*verlegen*	~~embar(r)as(s)ed~~
medi**e**v**a**l	*mittelalterlich*	~~medi(a)evel~~
misch**ie**vous	*spitzbübisch*	~~mischivous~~
ni**n**th	*neunte*	~~nineth~~

Exercise 3 Underline the mispelt word and correct it. There is one in each sentence.

1 John Baker is a good acquaintence of mine.

2 The idea of swopping homes can be attractive.

3 The forcast says it will reach 35°C today.

4 I developed this computer programme.

5 She reccomended some interesting books to me.

6 The Americans are somtimes accused of naivity.

7 Jane lives in a 35-story tower block.

8 Unfortunately, I came eigth in the race.

9 The tabloid press makes great use of exagerration.

10 The royal family was embarassed by the article.

11 Sexual harrasment is unlawful im most countries.

12 The British parlament is made up of two houses.

13 Do you know their holiday adress?

14 Do you know how many US presidents have been assasinated?

4 Gebrauch des Trennungsstrichs

① Jack is a very good football ~~play–er~~.
② Most people have the televion in the ~~liv–ing~~-room.
③ The United nations is the biggest ~~internatio–nal~~ organization.
④ Have you read Jane's ~~lett–er~~ yet?

✓ ❶ Jack is a very good football **player.**
✓ ❷ Most people have the television in the **living–room.**
✓ ❸ The United Nations is the biggest **inter–national** organization.
✓ ❹ Have you read Jane's **let–ter** yet?

→ Grundsätzlich können Sie ein mehrsilbiges Wort zwischen den Silben trennen, solange **mindestens zwei Buchstaben am Ende der ersten Zeile stehen** und – abgesehen von der Endsilbe -**ly** – es **mehr als drei Buchstaben am Anfang der nächsten** gibt. Beachten Sie, dass Sie wegen dieser Regel kurze zweisilbige Wörter wie **along**, **also**, **duet**, **player** usw. **nicht trennen** können, da es weniger als drei Buchstaben am Anfang der Folgezeile geben würde. Generell sollte man so viele Buchstaben wie möglich am Ende der ersten Zeile benutzen. Aus diesem Grund trennen wir zum Beispiel ein Wort wie **communist** so: **commun–ist**.

→ **Zusammengesetzte Wörter** wie **airport**, **baseball**, **motorway**, **dining-room**, **pop-singer**, **well-paid** usw. können nur zwischen den individuellen Wörtern getrennt werden: **air–port**, **base–ball**, **motor–way**.

→ Dieselbe Regel gilt für **Wörter mit Vor- bzw. Nachsilben**: **il–legal**, **inter–national**, **un–tidy**, **comfort–able**, **jump–ing**, **mis–understand–ing**.

→ Wörter mit einem Doppelbuchstaben wie **letter**, **putting**, **success**, können dazwischen getrennt werden: **let–ter**, **put–ting**, **suc–cess**.

Im Englischen wird die Worttrennung viel weniger gebraucht als es im Deutschen der Fall ist. In der Handschrift ist eine Trennung nur im Falle von wirklich langen Wörtern wie *controversial*, *exaggerated* und *international* gelegentlich nötig. Sonst ist es besser, größere Wortabstände zu benutzen, um eine Trennung völlig zu vermeiden.

Exercise 4 Imagine that these words come at the end of a line. Where could you split them? Mark words you cannot split with a cross (**x**).

☼	**postman**	________	5	swimming-pool	________
1	multinational	________	6	colour	________
2	runner	________	7	communist	________
3	legalise	________	8	Frenchman	________
4	yacht	________	9	tonne	________

B 14 Fehler durch falsche Kommasetzung

① Sarah ~~said, that~~ she couldn't ~~come, because~~ she had a cold.
② We went to ~~London, (in order)~~ to see a new musical.
③ The ~~dog, that~~ I saw, was a dachshund.
④ If it ~~rains we'll~~ eat indoors.
⑤ Please get some bread, ~~butter, and~~ tomatoes.
⑥ Jane ~~had luckily brought~~ her credit card with her.
⑦ John ~~said "Let's~~ meet at the weekend."

✓ ❶ Sarah **said that** she couldn't **come because** she had a cold.
✓ ❷ We went **to London (in order) to see** a new musical.
✓ ❸ The **dog that I saw was** a dachshund.
✓ ❹ **If** it **rains, we'll** eat indoors.
✓ ❺ Please get some bread, **butter and** tomatoes.
✓ ❻ Jane **had, luckily, brought** her credit card with her.
✓ ❼ John **said, "Let's** meet at the weekend."

→ Im Deutschen wird das Komma erheblich häufiger benutzt als im Englischen. Daher stellt die – im Englischen – unzulässige Anwendung des Kommas den Hauptfehler von deutschsprachigen Lernenden dar. Deswegen gilt generell die Regel: **When in doubt, leave it out.**

→ Im Gegensatz zum Deutschen, wird das **Komma** im Englischen in den folgenden Fällen **nicht gebraucht**:

Vor **bestimmenden Nebensätzen**, die mit that ❶, **what**, **how**, **where**, **who** usw. anfangen.

Vor **because** ❶, (**in order**) **to** ❷, **but** *(aber)*.

Bei **notwendigen** Relativsätzen ❸.

→ Im Englischen wird das **Komma gebraucht**:

Um **nicht-notwendige** Relativsätze abzutrennen.

In **if-Sätzen**, wenn der **if**-Teil an **erster Stelle** steht ❹.

In **Auflistungen**, außer vor **and** ❺.

Um „**Einschiebungen**" vom übrigen Satz abzutrennen ❻.

In der **direkten** Rede, nach dem einleitenden Verb ❼.

Um **Frageanhängsel** vom übrigen Satz abzutrennen.

Exercise 1 Insert commas only when absolutely necessary. Use a tick (✔) to show that a sentence is already correct.

1 Hemingway who was born in Chicago spent much of his life outside the USA.

2 The environment conference that was held in Brazil had little effect.

3 There would have been no crisis if we had acted more decisively.

4 The businessmen who visited our firm yesterday were from Korea.

5 The author mentions discrimination on the grounds of race sex religion and class.

6 If the Prime Minister loses the election he will retire from politics.

7 The referee told the player to leave the field.

8 The couple whose daughter was on TV last night are our next door neighbours.

9 You won't find the road that we live in on the map.

10 Abraham Lincoln was the first US president who was assassinated wasn't he?

11 The school which was only founded in 1977 now achieves the best exam results in the whole country.

C

Lösungen zu den Übungen

A 1

1
1 examines
2 flies, plays
3 goes, hopes
4 falls
5 focuses
6 approaches

2
1 summarizes, presents
2 employs, enable, experience
3 catches, achieves, deal with
4 points out, causes, reject, suffers

3
1 have finished, have now started
2 has been
3 have just tidied
4 have already written, have had
5 has attended, has always done
6 has still not passed, has had

4
1 The UK has asked the EU for more time to think about the new regulations about toxic emissions.
2 Unfortunately, the UK has used the Irish Sea as a chemical dump for years.
3 British firms have now agreed to fit the most modern filters to new factories.
4 Germany has not yet approved the export of nuclear waste to Russia.
5 Car makers have fitted catalytic converters to all new cars since 1990.
6 More efficient engines have led to big fuel savings.

5
1 did not write
2 is not, do not like
3 do not agree, do not seem, is not
4 do not go
5 has not introduced, do not want
6 did not find, does not mention

6
1 did the three newest members join the EU?
2 were the other members glad about this
3 would France and Germany like to see?
4 do they think this?
5 do Britain and Denmark want?

7
1 did he join
2 did he leave the Star
3 did he go to
4 did he go there
5 did he become an ambulance-driver
6 did he have to spend in hospital
7 did these insights lead him to write
8 did he produce his best work
9 did he become, during his later life
10 did he write in 1952
11 did he win the Nobel Prize
12 did he die

A 2

1 popular, wonderful, delicious, quickly, easily, thoroughly, clean, medium-sized, large, small, large, ready, roughly, gently, carefully, generously, slowly, approximately, regularly, necessary, gently, gradually, continuously, thoroughly, sure, freshly, fully, constantly, thick

2
1 boring, happier, more interesting
2 sure, more supportive, friendlier
3 most nationalist, more difficult
4 true, more tolerant, strictest, most traditional, huge, most awful
5 best, hard, better
6 more useful, wonderful

3
1 more carefully
2 more slowly, more easily
3 better, harder, more efficiently, longer
4 more seriously
5 more often, most frequently
6 more correctly, more fluently, more

4
1 The UK is smaller than Germany.
2 Roger has not got as many children as David.
3 The press report is much shorter than the essay.
4 The AX is just as good as the 204.

A 3

1
1 an, a
2 an, a
3 X, a
4 an, X, a
5 a
6 a, X, a

2
1 such a stupid remark
2 half an hour
3 rather a fool
4 What nonsense
5 quite a serious attack
6 rather a long time

3
1 Birgit was in a bad mood, so I left her in peace.
2 We worked ten hours without a break today.
3 Jochen is just coming. He is having a shower.
4 I have very little time. I'm in a great hurry.
5 All good things come to an end.
6 Why can't we go to the theatre for a change?

4
1 the, X, the, the, X
2 the, the, the, X
3 the, the, X, X, X, the, the, the, X, X, X, the, the

5
1 Religion still has a great influence on society.
2 A lot of Scots want independence from England.
3 Most minorities still feel disadvantaged.
4 Until recently South Wales was dependent on coal mining.
5 If governments are not willing to protect nature we will all die out.
6 In most EU countries children must go to school until they are 16.

A 4

1
1 The Harpers' garden
2 Gladys's husband
3 students' essays
4 Mrs Adams's bike
5 the children's playroom

2
1 the roof of the house
2 the discovery of America, the course of human history
3 his dad's car
4 head teacher of our school, Charles's mother.
5 the land of the blind
6 the owners of factories, the entrance of the works
7 animals' rights, "the assassins of nature".
8 the future of Europe, the success of the EU
9 tonight's TV guide, Jane's new play
10 the front of the queue

A 5

1
1 societies, minorities
2 churches, county
3 descriptions, lives, trenches
4 television, society
5 roofs, motifs
6 heroes

2
1 bars of
2 gallons of
3 crates of
4 tubes of
5 aerosols of, bar of
6 bottles of
7 tubs of

3
1 food, mice, flies
2 animal lovers, forced feeding, geese
3 Dentists, sweets, teeth, children
4 jobs, men, oil
5 series, soap operas
6 problem, hovercraft, aircraft, passengers, ship

4
1 In my opinion German youth is much better than its reputation.
2 Don't forget to bring a pair of pyjamas with you.
3 Business people must learn that people will not accept rising prices.
4 A policeman stopped three young men.
5 We need a pair of pliers to take out this part.
6 The peoples of the Sahara are among the poorest in the world.

5
1 information
2 news
3 furniture
4 pieces of furniture
5 pieces of evidence
6 piece of research

6
1 wolves
2 are
3 lives
4 is
5 aircraft
6 paint
7 pair of
8 chiefs

A 6

1
1 myself
2 me, me
3 yourself, me, him / her
4 you, yourselves
5 himself, them
6 Yourself
7 herself, her

2
1 E
2 R
3 R
4 E
5 E
6 R

3
1 myself
2 themselves
3 yourselves
4 herself
5 itself
6 himself / herself

4
1 has changed
2 sit down
3 introduced himself / herself
4 amuse themselves
5 will hurt yourself
6 to look after themselves
7 can help ourselves
8 note

5
1 herself
2 each other
3 herself
4 each other
5 themselves, ourselves, each other
6 each other
7 himself, himself
8 each other, yourself

6
1 this
2 those
3 that
4 That
5 these
6 this, That

A 7

1
1 any, some
some, any, some
2 any, any, some
any, some,
3 some, any
any

2
1 anybody, anywhere
something, somebody
2 something, some, some
anything,
3 anything, some
somewhere, somebody

3
1 We have got a lot of girls in our group, but not many boys.
2 Hurry up! We haven't got much time.
3 How much money should I get? We'll need a lot (of money) at the weekend.
4 You smoke too much, Mr Snow – and you shouldn't work so much, either.

4
1 A lot of, much
2 plenty of, much
3 a lot of, much, much
4 a lot of, much
5 a lot of, many, much
6 A lot of, much, a lot of, much
7 plenty of

5
1 little
2 Few, little
3 a few
4 few, a little, a few
5 a little
6 Few, little
7 a little

6
1 plenty of
2 a lot of
3 few
4 a little
5 (not) much
6 (not) many
7 some
8 a few
9 little
10 any
11 any
12 few
13 some

A 8

1
1 should be
2 May I borrow
3 Shall we collect
4 should not disturb
5 must go
6 could have

2
1 must
2 had to
3 Will I have to
4 has had to
5 must / has to
6 are going to have to

3
1 cannot
2 has not been able to
3 will be allowed to
4 Were they able to
5 Can
6 could not

4
1 needn't
2 must
3 needn't, must
4 mustn't
5 must

5
1 don't have to help
2 have to
3 doesn't have to, has to
4 X
5 have to

6
1 nicht kommen können, sich kümmern müssen
2 nicht rauchen sollten, sich nicht einigen können
3 haben können, besuchen möchten
4 nicht fahren dürfen, nicht fahren müssen
5 nicht tragen müssen, selbst entscheiden dürfen
6 anfangen sollen, nicht gehen dürfen

A 9

1
1 crime is ▼ caused
2 Hard punishment ▼ leads
3 increases sharply ▼.
4 I have ▼ read
5 shows us a video ▼.
6 We are ▼ asked to prepare

2
1 2, 1, 5, 3, 4
2 2, 4, 1, 3
3 6, 1, 2, 5, 3, 4, 7
4 4, 5, 2, 3, 6, 1
5 2, 1, 5, 3, 4
6 1, 7, 5, 4, 2, 6, 3

3
1 We can go soon. It has almost stopped raining.
2 Shakespeare was born in Stratford in 1564 but he spent most of his life in London.
3 Unfortunately, I must work next weekend.
4 It was still possible to play safely in the streets thirty years ago.
5 Surveys show clearly that a lot of older people are afraid to leave their homes at night.

4

Front-	Mid-	End-position manner	place	frequency / time
as a rule	always	angrily	at the party	at 10 am
luckily	often	fast	in Berlin	each summer
of course	seldom	noisily	in prison	every day
on the whole	sometimes	sadly	out of bed	every other night
(sadly)*				last Christmas
(sometimes)*				today
				twice a week

** können auch Satzadverb sein*

A 10

1
1 are reading
2 noticed
3 has been living
4 was doing
5 have seen
6 have been hearing / heard
7 have been waiting
8 is seeing

2
1 are arguing
2 is hoping
3 show, have, seem, are
4 give, have, is
5 says, is planning
6 am trying, keep
7 have got, are turning
8 does, is putting, doesn't trust, does

3
1 were doing, sounded, had to leave, was, returned, had, was searching, seems, was trying
2 got, came, was using, was, was sitting, did not see, put, turned, was standing
3 was driving, ran, didn't see, came, was driving, could stop, happened

4
1 Do you want to borrow my umbrella? It is raining.
2 I hurt my finger while I was preparing the vegetables.
3 How embarrassing. When we arrived the Snows were going to bed.
4 Unfortunately, I must go now. Somebody is waiting for me at the airport.
5 Olaf reads a lot of English books. He is reading a bestseller by John le Carré at the moment.

A 11

1
1 going to
2 will
3 will
4 going to
5 will

2
1 Tom and Mary are going to get a divorce.
2 We are not taking a holiday next year.
3 The firm is opening an office in Erfurt next month.
4 We are having a barbecue on Saturday.
5 The government is going to bring in a new law to control the use of drugs.
6 The education authorities are introducing new exams at the beginning of the next school year.

3
1 The weather forecast says (that) it will be sunny tomorrow.
2 My brother is flying to Florida on 10 August.
3 I can't come tomorrow. My train leaves at 11.30.
4 I suppose (that) we will get a good price for our flat.
5 Is Tom going to buy a new car?

A 12

1
1 There is something wrong with this sentence.
2 There was a big demonstration in Bonn yesterday.
3 There were a lot of people in town today.
4 It was very nice of you to drive me home.
5 Excuse me, please. Is there a filling-station near here?
6 Do you think there will also be questions on "Hamlet"?
7 It is difficult to share Peter's opinion on immigrants.
8 There are a lot of steaks left over. There is no point in buying more meat.

2
1 What
2 Who
3 Who
4 What
5 Which
6 Which

3
1 ... one, either.
2 ... idea, too.
3 ... the EU, too?
4 ... together, either.
5 ... so, either.
6 ... her, either.

4
1 a German newspaper, one
2 book, X
3 house, one
4 batteries, X
5 films, X
6 tomatoes, ones
7 jeans, X
8 restaurant, one

5
1 Each / Every
2 Each / Every
3 Each / Every, each
4 Each
5 each
6 Every

6
1 Ben
2 to them
3 the MPs
4 to us
5 to the meeting
6 the guests
7 the mechanic
8 to the authors
9 to customers
10 to his parents
11 me, to your wife
12 to Granny
13 the waiter

B 1

1
1 in an ugly way
2 loudly
3 in a silly way
4 in a cowardly way
5 slowly
6 thoroughly

2
1 older pedestrians, pretty seriously injured
2 hardly surprising, the poor, unjustly treated
3 freely, very closely
4 glad, nearly, this boring play
5 naturally, in a friendly way
6 a widely held view, big classes, the growing crisis
8 hard to deny, lately, powerless, really

3 most advanced, high-quality, nearly, important, close, high, secure, high, varied, performance-related, nearly, fast-developing, huge, daily, steadily

B 2

1

simple present:	present perfect:
always	all my life
day after day	before now
every Easter	for several weeks
from time to time	since I was a child
occasionally	so far this morning
regularly	the whole afternoon
seldom	up till this moment
usually	up to today

2
1 has lived, since her marriage
2 seldom, eats, has been, for months
3 always, prepare, never, asks
4 does not only do, has performed, during the last few seasons
5 When, have finished, can give
6 have spoken, several times, seems, now
7 can see, in a moment, has just arrived
8 have known, ever since she was a baby, haven't seen, for years

3
1 has not had, gave
2 worked, was, designed, built
3 wanted, has done, said, has introduced, have been
4 have you known, met, have seen
5 read, claimed, have had, has not improved, have managed, got
6 visited, left, happened, was, was

4
1 The Greggs have been arguing all morning again.
2 Mrs Coe has been living here ever since she was a little girl.
3 It has been raining for weeks now.
4 You have been sleeping for ages.
5 This novel is too long. We have been reading it now since the beginning of March.
6 The president has been governing by decree for over a year.

5
1 have not seen
2 have just passed
3 have been negotiating, have still not reached
4 has failed, has decided
5 have forbidden, have refused, have been marching
6 have not seen
7 has been living

B 3

1
1 d
2 e
3 a
4 b
5 f
6 c

2
1 That case is much too heavy. I will help you.
2 The author thinks that the government will change the law.
3 Do you think that privatization will lead to price increases?

3
1 Next July we will be visiting our relatives in the USA.
2 They will still be repairing the car at 3 o'clock.
3 I will be seeing Sean at the beginning of August.
4 Brenda will be collecting those statistics for months.
5 Will you be attending the meeting tomorrow?
6 Mr Carr will be asking your opinion within the next few days.
7 At this time tomorrow afternoon we will be driving through (to) Leeds.

4
1 East Germany will not have caught up with West Germany for another generation.
2 Will you have completed the job by 5 o'clock?
3 Sue will have worked here for 40 years at the end of the month.
4 Don't worry. You will definitely have received the new passport by then.

5
TOM: Are you doing
ANN: am going, am visiting
TOM: starts
ANN: will be, won't feel, are, will stay
TOM: will tell, will come, will meet
ANN: am not going to stand
TOM: will just stay

B 4

1
1 were immediately shown
2 has recently been suggested
3 had been formally opened
4 is tipped
5 are being decorated
6 cannot be created, must also be considered
7 has not really been taken
8 have been seriously divided
9 will be published

2 1 The "Grapes of Wrath" was written by Steinbeck, not (by) Hemingway.
2 Tickets can be bought at the main entrance.
3 Reference books should not be taken out of the library.
4 Computers are used to process all kinds of data.
5 The microchip was developed in the late 1960s.
6 The first modern computer was built by the University of Pennsylvania in 1946.
7 The testing of nuclear weapons is supported by very few people.
8 In case of breakdown, the manufacturers must be informed at once.

3 1 It was claimed that the crime rate is now falling.
2 It will be said by porn-dealers that customers just get what they want.
3 Private cars were found to be serious polluters.
4 It is believed by a few weird sects that the world will end in 2020.
5 Middle-class voters are said to be turning to Labour.
6 Hashish is said to be less dangerous than alcohol.

4 is; is paid; watch; is; is not spent; is; have probably not heard; is; have been put; Does that fact surprise; look at; are; has been shown; send; do; grew; had to be asked; had; was; had simply run out; have been built; have again started; suffer; has been pointed out; has increased; have been locked up; have been imprisoned; was investigated; was jailed; was told; had recently died; was confronted; was still sent; had to be taken; am; must be obeyed

B 5

1 1 seeing
2 to get
3 asking
4 closing
5 to spend
6 reading

2 1 Please don't forget to bring your sports things with you tomorrow.
2 Nobody can expect a woman to live with a violent husband.
3 Soloists must practise singing every day.
4 The firm admits exporting arms to Iraq.
5 The Prime Minister has decided to call an election in the autumn.
6 I wish Bob would stop telling such lies.

3 1 to telephone
2 to spend
3 having
4 working
5 to convince
6 visiting
7 to introduce
8 losing, becoming
9 celebrating

B 6

1 1 win, will be
2 spent, would be
3 will have to go, are not
4 would not have rioted, had shown
5 would start, abandoned
6 would not have signed, had understood

2 1 Will the government publish
2 Would the crisis have spread
3 Would Russia join
4 Will Labour win
5 Would the Republicans cut
6 Would Germany have reunited

3 1 will have to sell, does not find
2 had not acted, would have missed
3 increase, will lose
4 would be, was
5 do not restrict, will become
6 did not charge, would not have
7 would have not won, had voted

B 7

1 1 which; 2 whose; 3 which; 4 whom; 5 whose; 6 who

2 1 The policy helped blacks to get employment which was once just for whites.
2 It grew from the popular support people gave to the Civil Rights Movement.
3 This was the movement that was led by Martin Luther King.
4 Lyndon Johnson was the president who made affirmative action law.
5 It was a policy that always caused a great deal of argument.
6 There were Republicans who believed that it was undemocratic.

3 1 A survey ▾ was presented to the home secretary yesterday.
2 The survey, ▾, found that little has changed.
3 The results, ▾, make sad reading for women.
4 It was found that in Britain today it is still women ▾.
5 This applied to working women, ▾, as well.
6 The survey showed that even young men ▾ do not help much in the home.
7 While it was men ▾, women had to do all the routine jobs.
8 Isobel Hall, ▾, says couples should discuss the division of work honestly.
9 Above all, women, ▾, should not be automatically and unfairly disadvantaged.
10 English law, ▾, at least makes equality at work a legal requirement.
11 Equality is something ▾ but we have got a long way to go before it is reality.

B 8

1 1 Sally failed the exam in spite of having a lot of private lessons.
2 It is no good expecting me to live your life for you.
3 Instead of working, Jane spent her time dreaming of becoming an actress.
4 There is no alternative to learning these idioms by heart.
5 Our teacher has never given us the chance of discussing our own ideas.
6 Sarah has recently succeeded in selling several of her paintings.
7 It will not be worth repairing our old car again.
8 We are looking foward to receiving your answer shortly.
9 You will never train your dog by hitting him.

2
1 A lot of people are afraid of flying.
2 Unfortunately he has no experience of teaching adults.
3 You can't prevent people from thinking.
4 My day consisted of listening to endless speeches.
5 I am not used to being spoken to so rudely.
6 The lecturer began by telling us how clever she is.

3 reading; picking up; pleading; passing; fighting; Waiting; listening; looking; Taking; Coming; turning; opening; beating; holding; Kissing; Whispering; Removing; looking around; going about; Looking at; being caught; Lighting; smoking

B 9

1
1 The minister said that the government would take every possible step to ensure that consumption of beef was safe for our children.
2 Doctor Prowse said that they had discovered that the disease had occured in more areas than they had thought.
3 Joan French told the press that she thought the current situation had been made worse by the press who had not informed the population properly.
4 Amy Gardner said that they didn't eat beef in her family and that they hadn't done for years. She was quite sure that nothing would happen to her family.
5 Alex Butcher told us that he liked beef and that he would continue eating it. What was going on was just one big media hype.

2
1 Helen wanted to know what the role of the security council is.
2 Tony asked how many members the UN had had at the beginning.
3 Jane asked which countries are permanent members of the security council.
4 Mike enquired where the headquarters of the UN had been before it moved to New York.
5 Chris asked if / whether the director-general has to come from a neutral country.
6 Sarah wanted to know if the UN had lost any influence since the cold war.

3 1 accused; 2 doubts; 3 wondered; 4 argues; 5 advise; 6 pleaded

B 10

1 1 for; 2 for; 3 to; 4 about; 5 for; 6 about

2
1 differ
2 relied
3 advises
4 objecting
5 believe
6 succeed
7 approve

3
1 freedom from
2 interest in
3 anxiety about
4 awareness of
5 amazement at
6 worries about
7 Kindness to
8 marriage to

4
1 with, of
2 without
3 in
4 by
5 from, on
6 out of
7 at
8 on
9 at
10 to
11 by
12 In, to
13 on
14 for
15 In / Under

5
1 We can meet at my parents' in London.
2 Becker was Wimbledon champion at 17.
3 The police did nothing. They just laughed at me.
4 The journalist asked for an interview.
5 You should apologize for your bad behaviour.
6 The man has confessed to the crime.
7 I insist on your presence at the meeting.
8 We refer to your letter of 6 June.
9 I have little sympathy for the spoilt children of rich parents.
10 Society has an obligation to older people.
11 Ben told us about his journey at length.
12 In practice, such ideas are completely Utopian.

B 11

1
1 Look out
2 work out
3 stay up
4 give up
5 take off
6 find out
7 make out
8 put away
9 tried on
10 call out
11 will call in
12 pick up
13 are looking forward to
14 grew up

2
1 up
2 on
3 out
4 up
5 up
6 out, out
7 on, out
8 in
9 off
10 up
11 on, after
12 off
13 out
14 up, around

3
1 take on
2 carrying out
3 take off
4 looking into
5 tore up
6 given back
7 fix up
8 show off
9 put on
10 cleared up
11 left out
12 set off
13 put up with
14 got away
15 knocked down
16 stood up

B 12

1
1 Don't worry. The dog is usually good / well-behaved.
2 I haven't much time. Can you do the stairs?
3 In Islamic countries you should dress discreetlyy.
4 His pension isn't even sufficient to pay the rent.
5 I must take the children to school today.
6 A diet of crisps and biscuits is hardly healthy.
7 Unfortunately a lot of so-called "financial consultants" are not reputable.
8 A lot of restaurants offer a cheap set meal for tourists.
9 At first Markus seems unfriendly towards strangers.
10 How many states are there in the federal republic?
11 Prescriptions are no longer completely free to patients.
12 I think that Jane has become a very nice / pleasant woman.
13 The Germans donate more money than other Europeans.
14 It's a fact that talented people are also often sensitive people.
15 We want to buy a nice guest house.
16 Can I please have the most current edition of the time table.

2 1 practice, practising
2 lose, loose
3 lucky, happy
4 principle, principle, principal
5 get, get, become
6 ready, finished
7 cities, towns, towns, cities
8 lend, borrow
9 practicable, practical
10 lie, laying
11 industrious, industrial
12 receipt, recipe
13 variety, versatility
14 game, play
15 difficult, heavy, big
16 took place, occurred
17 advice, advise

3 1 evade
2 prescribe
3 biannual
4 economical
5 sociable
6 licence
7 repels
8 implying
9 definitive

4 1 land › state
2 laying › lying
3 effect › affect
4 happens › takes place
5 make a pause › have a break
6 decent › discreet / subdued
7 Eventually › Maybe
8 sensible › sensitive
9 wife › woman
10 remark › notice
11 adviced › advised
12 borrow › lend

B 13

1 1 permissible
2 edible
3 noticeable
4 likeable
5 sensible
6 unplayable
7 acceptable
8 visible
9 sizeable
10 responsible
11 hospitable
12 advisable
13 “audible”
14 legible
15 unpronounceable
16 reproducible

2 civilize; colonize; criticize; economize; emphasize; industrialize; legalize; organize; realize; recognize; standardize

3 1 acquaintence › acquaintance
2 swopping › swapping
3 forcast › forecast
4 programme › program
5 reccomend › recommend
6 naivity › naivety
7 35-story › storey
8 eigth › eighth
9 exagerration › exaggeration
10 embarassed › embarrassed
11 harrasment › harassment
12 parlament › parliament
13 adress › address
14 assasinated › assassinated

4 1 multi-national
2 run-ner
3 legal-ize
4 X
5 swimming-pool
6 col-our
7 commun-ist
8 French-man
9 X

B 14

1 1 Hemingway, who was born in Chicago, spent much of his life outside the USA.
2 The environment conference that was held in Brazil had little effect. ✔
3 There would have been no crisis if we had acted more decisively. ✔
4 The businessmen who visited our firm yesterday were from Korea. ✔
5 The author mentions discrimination on the grounds of race, sex, religion and class.
6 If the prime minister loses the election, he will retire from politics.
7 The referee told the player to leave the football field. ✔
8 The couple whose daughter was on TV last night are our next door neighbours. ✔
9 You won’t find the road that we live in on the map. ✔
10 Abraham Lincoln was the first US president who was assassinated, wasn’t he?
11 The school, which was only founded in 1977, now achieves the best exam results in the whole country.

Bildnachweis

Zeichnungen: alle außer auf Seite 31 und 44 von Christine Georg; Zeichnung S. 44 Carlos Borrell.
Photos: S. 10: Archiv für Kunst und Geschichte, Berlin; S. 13 Marion Schweitzer, München; S. 23 Bavaria Bildagentur, Düsseldorf; S. 47 J. Allan Cash Ltd, London; S. 68 Bavaria Bildagentur, Düsseldorf; S. 71 Marion Schweitzer, München; S. 77 Fotoagentur Zentralbild GmbH, Berlin; S. 87 Bavaria Bildagentur, Düsseldorf; S. 99 Bavaria Bildagentur, Düsseldorf; S. 105 Bildarchiv Engelmeier, München; S. 112 dpa, Frankfurt.